ST. JOSEPH'S COLLEGE OF EDUCATION LIBRARY

This book is issued in accordance with current College
Library Regulations.

DATE DUE AT LIBRARY LAST STAMPED BELOW

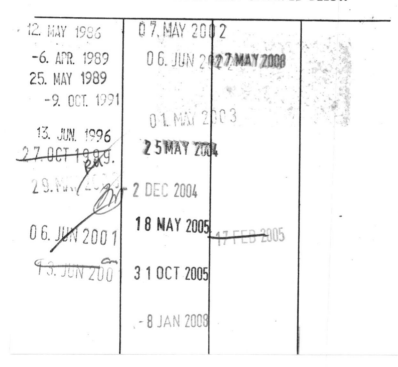

Gymnastics:
A Mechanical Understanding

Gymnastics:
A Mechanical Understanding

Tony Smith

HODDER AND STOUGHTON
LONDON SYDNEY AUCKLAND TORONTO

British Cataloguing in Publication Data

Smith, Tony
  Gymnastics.
  1. Gymnastics—Physiological aspects
  2. Human mechanics
  I. Title
  612'.76   GV461

ISBN 0 340 28164 2 Boards
ISBN 0 340 28165 0 Paperback

First published 1982

Illustrations by Tony Evans and Meg Warren

Printed and bound in Great Britain for
Hodder and Stoughton Educational,
a division of Hodder and Stoughton Ltd,
Mill Road, Dunton Green, Sevenoaks, Kent,
by Richard Clay (The Chaucer Press) Ltd, Bungay, Suffolk

Typeset by Macmillan India Ltd, Bangalore

Contents

Foreword

The foremost difficulty in producing this text is that of striking a balance between technical rigour and gymnastic intelligibility. It is one thing to write an accurate treatise on relevant mechanics, another to make it readable by the average gymnastic coach, who may not have a particularly deep mathematical or mechanical background. Indeed, in striving for a mid-point Tony Smith has had to suffer the oscillations between the two extremes as represented by the two writers of this Foreword. The result is a book that should appeal to all thoughtful coaches – written by a man who has experienced to the full the workings of an amateur Governing Body of sport and a number of academic and educational institutions. He is a club coach, a national squad coach, a servant to many gymnastic committees and lecturer at a number of national Conferences. With this background plus his professional and academic standing he has created a book which will answer all questions relative to his subject within the scheme of work and syllabus of any coaching award. This book will also be invaluable to students of Physical Education as well as prospective coaching award candidates.

Using an excellent set of figurines and illustrations, the author leads the readers through a well-planned set of gymnastic examples covering the basic mechanical principles relevant to both Men's and Women's Gymnastics.

Tony Smith was requested to write this book because of his great contribution to the development of the sport of Gymnastics in Great Britain.

Paul Barnes, Ph.D.
Chairman, Men's Judging
Panel,
  British Amateur Gymnastics
  Association
  Member of B.A.G.A. Men's
  Technical Committee
International judge
Lecturer in Physics, Birkbeck
  College, University of London

John Atkinson
Director of National Training
  (Men and Boys), British
  Amateur Gymnastics
  Association

Preface

Gymnastics is undoubtedly the most technically complex of all modern sports. This, while being part of the compulsive attraction it has to offer, imposes considerable demands on coaches and performers. The range and depth of knowledge required for a full appreciation of the sport is formidable. In addition to a thorough understanding of the methodology of gymnastic moves, their classification and appropriate deductions, the coach's knowledge must also embrace such disciplines as physiology, anatomy, psychology and body mechanics. These are all essential areas of knowledge for the coach to be able fully to appreciate the total gymnastic picture. They all have an important part to play in producing the desired result, perfection of gymnastic movement.

The author's intention in writing this book is to improve coaching performance by increasing coaches' knowledge of the fundamental principles of body movement, and to show how these are related to moves on all pieces of gymnastic apparatus.

Body mechanics or biomechanics has until recently been a sadly neglected area of study, but now we find more attention is being focused on this important aspect of gymnastic knowledge. This is reflected in the increasing number of articles being published in this field. More information is now becoming available, but unfortunately, this is fragmented and often presented in too technical a form to be of any real value to gymnastic coaches.

Observation suggests that most gymnastic coaches come from one of four categories: past performers, physical educationists, Mums and Dads, and a final less clearly definable group having no apparently obvious reason for their involvement in the sport – indeed, many do not even know why they have allowed their lives to be completely taken over by this obsession called gymnastics.

To have any impact on gymnastic coaching on a broad front, and hence to be of any real value to gymnastic development, this book must cater for the needs of all these groups of coaches, a task which is clearly impossible without compromises. So some of the explanations of scientific principles have been simplified so that readers without a scientific background can understand their meanings.

Frequently, assumptions made in the text mean that justifiable criticism by biomechanics experts could be levelled at some of the over-simplifications that are adopted. This has been done deliberately, to ensure that the principle or principles being presented and developed are not lost in the confusion of a mass of detail.

There is now a growing awareness that the approach to the sport of gymnastics must become more scientifically based. Traditionally accepted methods of coaching gymnastic moves are being constantly queried and challenged. Intuitive coaching is slowly being replaced by analysis and scientific study. It is the opinion of this author that this trend will accelerate in the future. The complexity of new moves now being attempted, with the associated high levels of risk involved, will make this essential. Indeed, in many cases the analysis and study will have to be carried out to establish the feasibility of moves before they are even taken into the gymnasium.

It must be stressed that this book is not intended to be an in-depth study of the scientific analysis of human movement. It should be regarded by coaches as a starting point in the process of understanding and analysing the mechanical principles that govern gymnastic movements. Thus it is designed to provide a platform of basic knowledge which it is hoped will benefit the coach in the following ways:

1 It will provide a deeper understanding of the factors that influence and govern the correct execution of a gymnastic move.
2 It will provide a scientific background that will enable the coach to derive a deeper understanding of the ever-increasing number of technical articles and papers being published.
3 It will help to produce a scientific attitude to the coaching and analysis of gymnastic moves.

Coaching is primarily a visual art and a coach is only as good as his/her gymnastic eye. Coaches at the top level have educated their eyes through years of observation of top class performers. Gymnastics is primarily about body positions, body angles, body shapes and body movements, and the coach's eye must be trained to recognise what represents correct and incorrect body attitudes. Technically desirable body attitudes are positions which are also mechanically correct. For example, 'Straight legs, point your toes' are probably the most frequently used words in gymnasiums. Coaches, if asked 'Why?' by the inexperienced gymnast, might reply, 'It is unaesthetic not to keep the legs straight and the toes pointed', or 'The judges do not approve of and will deduct marks for bent legs and unpointed toes.' There is a third reason: this is the correct and most efficient leg position in mechanical terms for most gymnastic movements.

In attempting to improve readers' knowledge of the application of mechanical principles to gymnastic moves, we are at the same time attempting to train the eye of the gymnastic coach. Thus the reader should at each stage attempt to relate the principles presented to a visual impression of the correct body position required. This is most important for coaches who do not have the opportunity of regularly watching good performers. For this reason, each section of the book is devoted to the development of a mechanical principle or set of principles and contains examples which relate developed principles to selected gymnastic moves. Further to reinforce the process, each section concludes with a set of questions designed to stimulate the reader to apply the concepts presented to a wide range of gymnastic movements, the purpose being to encourage coaches to re-examine familiar moves in a different light, and to develop an attitude of mind such that when presented with a gymnastic move to coach the first reaction of the coach will be to examine that move in terms of correct mechanical requirements. This is of fundamental importance, as the correct mechanical requirements of a move dictate the physical requirements of the gymnast in terms of strength and mobility.

Many of the diagrams and ideas presented in this book have been used during gymnastic sessions with young gymnasts (10–14-year-olds) to explain the skills that are being taught. Experience has shown that some gymnasts are not only capable of appreciating but often of understanding the fundamental mechanics principles governing the moves. Consequently, it is the opinion of the author that such gymnasts should be exposed to these ideas at an early stage of their gymnastic career, so that they develop a scientific understanding of and approach to the sport. Coaches are therefore encouraged to introduce the terminology and principles of mechanics into the training of appropriate gymnasts. We are not only training today's gymnasts but perhaps also tomorrow's coaches.

Acknowledgments

Although the study of the mechanics of gymnastics' moves has been the focus of my attention for several years, without the initiative of Mr John Atkinson, Director of National Training for Men's and Boys' Gymnastics, British Amateur Gymnastics Association, this book would never have been started. Furthermore, he has been a constant source of advice and encouragement throughout its compilation.

I am also particularly indebted to Dr Paul Barnes, Convenor of the Men's Judging Panel of the British Amateur Gymnastics Association, and Mr Mike Holliday of the Department of Physical Education and Sports Science, University of Technology, Loughborough, for their invaluable comments at the draft stage of the book.

I record my appreciation of the work done by Mr Tony Evans and Mrs Meg Warren in producing the diagrams for the book.

Finally, my grateful thanks to my wife Sally for producing the typescript and for her invaluable help in proof reading.

Bridgend, 1982   *Tony Smith*

This book is recommended reading for all gymnastic coaches by the Men's and Women's Technical Committees of the British Amateur Gymnastics Association and has received the seal of approval of the Board of Control of the Association.

Introduction

This book is primarily concerned with the identification and study of mechanics principles and their application to the analysis of gymnastic movements. Mechanics can be defined as 'the study of the fundamental principles which govern, predict and explain the way in which a body will react to an applied force or forces': that is, the study of cause and effect. The cause or causes, we will show later, take the form of forces and/or turning moments applied to the gymnast, to produce the desired effect of correct body position and/or body movement, including flight and rotation. In the Preface, this statement is made: 'Gymnastics is primarily about body positions, body angles, body shapes and body movements . . .' Therefore the normal mechanics process of simply studying cause and effect would be incomplete without a brief consideration and appreciation of the agencies that are responsible for creating the body angles and movements necessary for the successful completion of the gymnastic skill being performed.

Kinesiology is the name given to the scientific study of human movement and embraces aspects of the following three disciplines:

1 *Biomechanics*, or the application of the principles of mechanics to the study of human movement;
2 *Anatomy*, which involves a study of the musculoskeletal system of the body and is the mechanical system responsible for body movement;
3 *Physiology*, which includes the study of the neuromuscular system of the body which is the system responsible for initiating, monitoring and controlling body movement.

The first chapter of the book is devoted to providing a basic understanding of the relevant aspects of the neuromuscular and musculoskeletal system – that is, an understanding of how the required body shapes and movements for gymnastic skills are formed. The rest of the book is concerned with the mechanical analysis of gymnastic moves.

There are many different ways in which a book on gymnastics can be structured. The most common presentation is a classification and presentation of information related to individual pieces of apparatus. Other presentations are through a progression of the difficulties of elements or 'genealogical trees' of gymnastic moves. The presentation of information in this book is designed so that each chapter develops a mechanics principle or set of principles and then relates the information to study and understanding of gymnastic moves. For example, Chapter 2, on the centre of gravity, is followed by Chapter 3 on force and turning moments (the causes of body movements). A consideration of body movements follows in Chapter 4 (the effects produced by the causes previously discussed). The way in which cause and effect relate to one another is then studied in Chapter 5, on force and motion. This leads logically to a study of forms of energy and their relevance to gymnastic moves. The book then concludes with a consideration of biomechanics studies, aimed at integrating and relating all the ideas previously developed.

A cursory examination of the text will reveal that it contains some formulae and many analyses of gymnastic moves. The non-mathematical reader should not be put off by this, because in the majority of instances an understanding of the coaching significance of the final results obtained is as important as understanding the mathematical processes used to achieve them.

The study of a gymnastic move using the principles of mechanics will determine the correct body attitudes and movements necessary for its successful execution. However, the body shapes and movements must be within the physical capabilities of the gymnast, in terms of mobility to provide the necessary range of movement and of strength to produce the relative movements and accelerations of different parts of the body. The agencies responsible for causing these movements are now considered.

List of Symbols

m	mass of gymnast
W	weight of gymnast
M	momentum of gymnast
G	centre of gravity
F	force
R	resultant force
v_x	horizontal velocity component
v_y	vertical velocity component
u	initial or starting velocity
v	final velocity
a	acceleration
g	acceleration due to gravity
T, t	time taken to complete move (also tension)
s	distance travelled by gymnast
h	distance of G (centre of gravity) from point of rotation
ω	angular velocity
θ	angle turned through or release angle
α	angular acceleration
I	moment of inertia
k	radius of gyration

1

Fundamental, Anatomic and Physiological Aspects of the Human Body

The Musculoskeletal System

This, as the name implies, is the arrangement of bones and muscles within the human body. The human frame is an extremely complex mechanism containing over 200 bones of which 177 are capable of relative movement. The movement of one bone relative to another is effected by a *force* applied by a muscle or group of muscles. A force is normally defined as 'a push or a pull which when applied to a body will cause or try to cause body movement to occur'. Here this definition must be modified, as the force applied by a muscle is always a pulling force because muscles are not rigid, and therefore incapable of producing a pushing action. The movement of one bone relative to the next occurs at the joint and the muscle that spans the

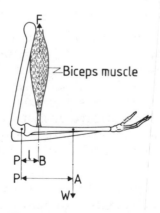

Figure 1 The arm as an anatomical lever

joint provides the motive force necessary. This is illustrated in Fig. 1, which shows the action of the biceps muscle which contracts or shortens in length to provide relative movement between the lower (radius and ulna) and upper (humerus) parts of the arms, the movement occurring through the elbow joint. In mechanics this mechanism is called a *lever*. A lever is a solid bar which is pivoted at a fixed point known as a *fulcrum* in such a way that the bar will rotate about the fulcrum if a force is applied to it at a specified point. In Fig. 1, if the humerus remains stationary, then the forearm (radius and ulna) would be the solid bar, the elbow joint the fulcrum, and the force F applied by the muscle to the lever at a distance l from the fulcrum, lifting the forearm of weight W. The system therefore forms an anatomical lever.

As a muscle can only pull, it is obvious that having caused relative movement of two bones to occur through the contraction of a muscle (or group of muscles), the opposite movement, a return to the original body position, requires the contraction of a different set of muscles. In the case of the arm movement shown in Fig. 1, this would require a contraction of the triceps muscle.

The muscle directly responsible for effecting the movement is called the *prime mover* (e.g. the biceps muscle in arm flexion), and the *antagonist* is the name given to the muscle which causes the opposite movement to the mover (e.g. the triceps muscle in arm extension). Clearly, both sets of muscles do not function simultaneously in causing movement. When a prime mover contracts to produce movement, the antagonist relaxes automatically and vice versa.

Classification of Levers

From the above example, it is clear that three things must be identified in order to be able to specify a lever completely:

(a) the point about which rotation occurs, the fulcrum;

(b) the point at which the effort is applied to the lever by the musular contraction (for complete specification, the magnitude and direction of the force should also be known);

(c) the point at which the resistance to movement (or weight) of the lever is applied or concentrated. In gymnastics, this will often be the weight of the limb being rotated, which is assumed to be concentrated at the *centre of gravity* of the limb. (See Chapter 2 for more detail.)

As there are three elements to a lever, there are three possible arrangements of these elements, and hence levers can be classified into three distinct groups. All three types of levers occur in the human body, and as the type of lever affects the efficiency of movement, it is important that the coach is able to distinguish between them.

1   In a *first order lever*, the fulcrum lies between the point of application of the effort (being supplied by the muscle) and the resistance point (being supplied by the weight of the anatomical lever).

2   In a *second order lever*, the resistance point lies between the fulcrum and the effort point.

3   In a *third order lever*, the effort lies between the fulcrum and the resistance point.

These different types of levers are illustrated in Fig. 2 and the following are common every-day examples:
First order: a pair of scissors, a crowbar, a see-saw
Second order: a wheelbarrow, the action of closing a door by means of the handle
Third order: the action of closing a door by pushing near the hinge

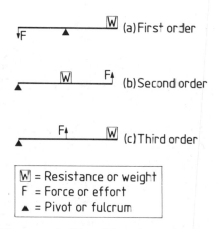

Figure 2 Classification of levers

ANATOMIC LEVERS

The use of the triceps muscle for arm extension is a good example of a first order anatomic lever. This is illustrated by the arrangement shown in Fig. 3. The force F is being supplied by the triceps muscle to move the weight W. The pivot point or fulcrum P (the elbow joint) is located between the effort and the resistance. This situation can be directly related to the type 1 lever shown in Fig. 2(a). With this type of lever, a small movement of the effort F causes a large movement of the resistance W. However, in life we don't get

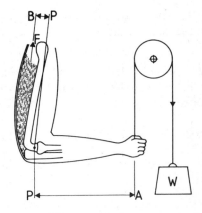

Figure 3 First order anatomic lever

anything for nothing. To compensate for this, the effort F must be greater than the resistance W, the ratio of F to W being the same as the ratio of the distance moved by W to the distance moved by F.

$$\text{i.e. } \frac{F}{W} = \frac{\text{AP}}{\text{BP}}$$

This will become clearer after reading Chapter 3 on force.

There are extremely few examples of second order levers in the human body, the most easily recognisable being the foot and ankle where the foot is being used to raise the body on to the toes. If we assume the fulcrum P to be at the point of contact of the foot with ground, then the effort F supplied to the foot at the heel where the achilles tendon is attached is outside the resistance W supplied by the weight of the gymnast. This is shown in Fig. 4 and can be

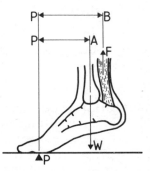

Figure 4 Second order anatomic lever (*Note*: In turning about the ankle joint this may be regarded as a first order lever with the ankle joint as fulcrum.)

compared directly with the type 2 lever shown in Fig. 2(b). Here it can be seen that a larger movement is required in the effort F to produce a smaller movement in the resistance W, and conversely the effort required is smaller than the value of the resistance to be overcome—a reverse situation to the previous one. The following relationship again holds:

$$\frac{F}{W} = \frac{AP}{BP}$$

Flexing of the forearm by contracting the biceps muscles is a good example of a third order lever. This has already been illustrated in Fig. 1. In this case, the effort is applied at a point between the fulcrum and the resistance. Hence the effort supplied must be considerably larger than the resistance to be overcome, but the distance moved by the effort is considerably less than the distance through which it moves the resistance. Again:

$$\frac{F}{W} = \frac{AP}{BP}$$

Now compare and relate the anatomical lever shown in Fig. 1 with the lever shown in Fig. 2(c).

Joints

The function of the joint is to allow relative movement between bones to occur. However, *joint stability* is also required. There are two aspects of joint stability:

(*a*) Resistance to displacement in a direction contrary to the normal range of movement of the joint;

(*b*) holding function, to 'lock' a joint in a desired position. This would be associated with static balance position in gymnastics.

Stability can be provided in different ways. *Ligaments* play an important part in joint stability. Ligaments are strong fibrous tissues which are attached to the ends of the bones of a movable joint and help to maintain the bones in correct relationship to each other. For example, the lateral ligaments of the knee help to prevent sideways movements which the joint is not designed to produce. The muscular arrangement around the joint, in addition to providing the motive force, also contributes to joint stability, particularly in joints whose structure itself does not greatly contribute towards this, e.g. plane joints. *Facia* also contribute to joint stability. These are fibrous tissues which either form sheaths for individual muscles, or partitions between muscles or smaller partitions which separate bundles of fibres within the muscle itself (depending on their location), and can range from thin membranes to tough fibrous sheets.

The shapes of the joint itself is an important consideration, e.g. ball and socket joints offer stability and the deeper the recess in the socket, the more stable the joint. For this reason, the hip joint is more stable than the shoulder joint, both being of the ball and socket type. However, this imposes a greater restriction on the range of movement of the hip joint.

The smooth movement of joints is facilitated by a separation of the moving surfaces by an intervening smooth substance such as glassy cartilage or fibrous tissues. Furthermore, almost all joints in the human skeleton are synovial (lubricated by synovial fluid) and this greatly assists smooth movement.

The musculoskeletal system of the body can now be regarded as a combination of lever mechanisms of immense complexity which makes possible the highly complex body movements required for the successful execution of gymnastic skills.

RANGE OF MOVEMENT

There are several factors that are related to the range of movement of joints. They include the type of joint, the shape of the surfaces, and the restraining effects of ligaments, muscles and tendons. It is not the purpose of this book to provide a basic text in anatomy and readers are advised to supplement this appreciation by referring to standard texts on anatomy (and through observation of living subjects and even of a skeleton if possible). For a detailed study and classification of the types of joints in the human body, see Wells and Luttgens, 1976 (in bibliography).

Range of movements of joints can be improved through the use of carefully selected exercises, but these should be done under controlled conditions. It is important that the improvements effected are capable of being measured and recorded. A simple method suitable for gymnasiums is the use of the British Amateur Gymnastics Association's (B. A. G. A.) suppling sheets, where range of movements is visually assessed by the coach and a mark is scored by the gymnast for each exercise, depending on the range of movement achieved. Fig. 5 shows a typical example where the flexion of the leg is being measured and scored.

A more precise method of measuring the range of movement of a joint is to measure (in degrees) the angle moved through from the starting position to that of maximum movement θ. Two instruments are commonly used for this purpose, the *goniometer* which is a protractor with two arms, one being stationary and the other moving (see Fig. 6(a)) and the *Leighton Flexometer* (Fig. 6(b)) which is a measuring instrument based on gravity and is capable of 360° measurement.

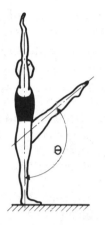

Figure 5 From B.A.G.A. strength and suppling sheets

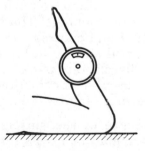

(a) Double arm Goniometer

(b) Leighton Flexometer

Figure 6 Range of movement measuring devices

Exercises for increasing the range of movement of joints can be broadly classified under three categories:

(a) *Exercises using the force of gravity.* A good example is splits training where the gymnast, after achieving the maximum stretch he/she is capable of, allows gravity to act on the body and further increase the range of movement.

(b) *Exercises using momentum.* In the above splits example, this would constitute bouncing gently up and down, i.e. using the momentum (mass times velocity) of the body to aid the stretching process. Other examples of using body momentum include arm circling and leg swinging.

(c) *Exercises against a resistance.* This may be a force applied by a partner, or a self-administered force applied by the gymnast. A typical example of working against a resistance is partner working to increase the range of movements, where the partner assists the leg lifting process to increase leg flexion.

To summarise, the range of movements of joints of a gymnast are limited not only by the bone structure but also by facia, ligaments and muscles, but can be increased by stretching of these elements by the use of carefully selected exercises. However, it should be stressed that these should only be carried out after warm-up activities have taken place, as this minimises the danger of pulls and tears and increases range of movement. It should be noted that improvements in range of movement will be lost if the exercises are discontinued.

Strength

Strength can be defined simply as the ability of the body to produce a force. This we have already stated, is produced by the shortening or contracting of a muscle, or group of muscles, which will cause movement to occur at the joint over which the muscle passes.

Muscles are composed of thousands of small fibres ranging in length from fractions of a millimetre (mm) to several centimetres, but only about 0.25 mm in thickness. The majority of the skeletal muscles are longitudinal and contraction therefore occurs along the longitudinal or central axis as shown in Fig. 7 (i.e. the fibres contract at 90° to the direction of pull).

The strength of a muscular contraction, and hence the force applied, depends on several factors, the most important being:

(a) the number and size of the muscle fibres (this obviously relates to the size of the muscle, i.e. its cross-sectional area);

(b) the ability to use as many of the muscle fibres as possible. If a muscle fibre is stimulated, it contracts to its maximum. Hence a

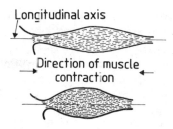

Figure 7 Muscle shortening along longitudinal axis

muscle fibre is either working or not; there is no intermediate stage. This is known as the 'all or none' principle.

Exercises for increasing strength can be grouped into three categories, *isotonic, isometric* and *isokinetic*, and are all based on the principle of overload. This involves working against a resistance. By gradually increasing the resistance against which muscles contract, there will be a gradual increase in strength. For maximum effect, the muscles must either overcome a maximum resistance or contract at a maximum speed.

Isotonic exercises involve the movement of weights through a specified distance and direction, curls with dumbells being an exercise specifically to strengthen the biceps muscles, squats to develop leg strength, and so on. A cautionary note, however, for coaches, especially those concerned with young children. Correct handling of weights is a specialised art and the injudicious use of weight exercises can be dangerous. A safer situation is to use multigym training facilities where there is no danger of weights being 'dropped'. Exercises against spring or elastic resistance also comes into this category, muscular contraction against a system providing a resistance.

Isometric exercises involve muscular contractions against a resistance which is immovable or simply too large to overcome. There are some popular misconceptions regarding isometric exercises. The sole purpose of these exercises is to increase muscular strength. It is not an effective method for improving physical fitness as it does not increase cardiovascular endurance or flexibility. The immovable resistance may be applied by a partner, a typical example being leg lifting (or lowering) against the resistance of a partner. Evidence suggests that isometric exercises are particularly beneficial for strengthening muscles or muscle groups that have been weakened through injury to joints. Isometric exercises which have been carefully selected prove an effective method of increasing muscle strength.

Isokinetic exercise differs from the above, in that it involves the control of the speed of muscular contraction instead of distance or resistance. In this type of exercise, the resistance is varied to accommodate the changing capability of the muscle at each point in the range of movement. Isokinetic equipment is expensive to purchase and not practical for gymnastic strength training. However, isokinetic principles can be applied to modify familiar exercises. This involves identification of the range of movement which vigorously stimulates the muscle being strengthened, and concentrating the exercise in that narrow range of movement. A good example would be the curl up exercises where the abdominal muscles are only strongly activated in the first 30° of the body elevation, when the resistance is virtually constant (that is, the moment of the body will only vary marginally). The reader will have a clearer understanding of this after reading Chapter 3 which discusses the principle of turning moments.

Again as with range of movement in measurement of strength it is important to record progress, and to use the results as a basis for evaluating the effectiveness of a strength training programme. Simple tests used to evaluate the overall strength of gymnasts are presented in the B. A. G. A. strength and mobility sheets and include press-ups, chins and leg lifts. Although there is no disputing the usefulness of these tests as a means of assessing and monitoring the general condition of gymnasts, a great deal of care should be used in their application. I recently witnessed a simple demonstration of a young gymnast who claimed to be able to do ten leg lifts. It was discovered that when the shoulders of the gymnast were prevented from moving backwards during the exercise, the gymnast could not raise the legs above the horizontal position. The gymnast had been raising the legs previously by using the chest and shoulder muscles and not exercising the muscles the exercise is designed to strengthen. Hence the standardisation of conditions is essential when using tests of this nature.

The above B.A.G.A. tests are tests of how many repetitions are achieved by the gymnast; for accurate strength measurement the magnitude of the force should be measured. Weights and multigym facilities can be used for this purpose, when the effort being applied can be measured directly in kilograms or pounds.

Dynamometers can also be used to measure force. These are devices used to measure directly the magnitude of an applied force, and are usually mechanical in nature where the deflection of, say, a spring represents the force applied and this is recorded on a scale graduated to represent force. For example, straight arm press exercises are important for developing strength in the muscle groups used for kips (upstarts) and uprises, and so on. These exercises can be made more interesting and competitive for the

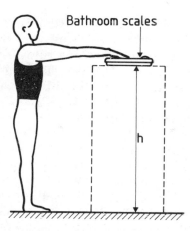

Figure 8 Use of scales as a simple force dynamometer

gymnast, and more informative for the coach, by adopting the training situation shown in Fig. 8, where the gymnast is pressing down on bathroom scales with straight arms. Weighing scales are, in fact, very simple dynamometers. In normal use, they measure the weight (force) exerted by a person due to the attractive force of earth's gravity. This force will obviously act vertically downwards. They are very useful devices in the gymnasium for measuring strength. Beware however, of the limitations of the situation shown. This will only measure the pressing strength of the gymnast for this specific position. The coach requires information regarding press strength within the total range of movement. This information can be obtained quite easily by varying the height h of the scales above the floor. In this way, weaknesses within the range of movement can be discovered, and strength training programmes can be designed to remedy shortcomings.

Measurement and recording of grip strength is an important factor in determining the ability of gymnasts to work advanced moves on the bars where large forces tending to throw the gymnast away from the bar are encountered (see Chapter 5). Specially designed grip dynamometers are commercially available, but again the bathroom scales can be effectively employed here (Fig. 9). These

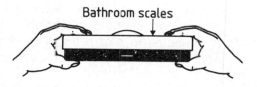

Figure 9 Use of scales as a grip dynamometer

are just two simple examples of how strength training can be made more interesting and informative using very simple cheap equipment. Coaches can develop situations relevant to their strength training programme in a similar way. There is no incentive like success or improvement, but realisation of success in strength improvement implies continual measurement and comparison of achievements. A cautionary note, though: all testing should be carried out under what is called 'controlled conditions'. By this, we mean that meaningful comparisons can only be made from tests carried out under identical conditions. If we refer back to the straight arm press strength measurements, the height settings must be the same for each set of tests. The distance the gymnast stands away from the scales should be the same. The physical condition of the gymnast taking the tests should be as near identical as possible. For example, there would be little value testing a gymnast on one occasion at the start of a session when fresh, and perhaps a week later at the end of a gruelling session. Only by standardising our test conditions are we able to make relevant comparisons and obtain useful information.

The Neuromuscular System

The following is a brief consideration of the aspects of the neuromuscular system that are relevant to our study of body movement. The interested reader is referred to any basic text on physiology for a fuller treatment of this subject.

Body movement occurs when muscular contraction causes movement of the skeletal framework of the body. The skeletal muscles respond to signals transmitted through the nervous system by way of the motor nerves. A muscle will remain relaxed unless it receives such a signal. The signal provided to the muscle is a response to the need of creating the body movement required by the gymnast for the execution of the skill being performed. Therefore, it is necessary that the central nervous system of the body is constantly receiving signals from the surroundings, so that it can continually appraise the movements it is generating, compare these with the correct movements for the execution of the skill, and make whatever adjustments are necessary. Hence the neuromuscular system forms what is known as a closed loop feedback mechanism. It is constantly delivering signals to muscles to cause body movement to occur, while at the same time constantly appraising and monitoring the effects of the movement, comparing with the desired ideal results and correcting for any errors or deviations that may have occurred.

This process is facilitated by means of *neurons*: *sensory neurons* which monitor, measure and appraise, and *motor neurons* which activate a muscular response. Additionally, there are *connector neurons* which exist completely within the central nervous system and, as their name implies, serve as connecting links.

Sensory nerve endings respond to stimuli. These can be divided into two main groups:

(a) those that receive stimuli from outside the human body, called *exteroceptors*, and which obviously include the five senses, sight, hearing, smell, touch and taste. These generate and transmit impulses as a result of stimulation.

(b) those that are adapted to respond to internal changes, called *enteroceptors*.

The most important sensory nerve endings from the point of view of body movement study are those known as *proprioceptors*, that is sensory elements that receive impulses from joints, tendons, muscles, ligaments, and so on. The proprioceptors are responsible for transmitting a constant flow of information from these body elements, regarding (for example) position rate and direction of movement of the organs concerned, to the central nervous system (*via* the spinal cord) for analysis. This information is transmitted as a series of nerve impulses.

Similar impulses are then passed back to the motor neuron units (the functional units of the neuromuscular system), each of which consists of a single motor neuron together with the muscle fibres it activates. The number of muscle fibres activated by one motor unit varies from under 100 to over 1,000, and this affects precision of movement. The lower the ratio of fibres to motor neurons, the greater the precision of movement.

One of the main requirements in gymnastics is the ability of the gymnast to respond quickly to stimuli. This is frequently called reaction time, or more precisely *response initiation time*. This process will involve the receipt and analysis of the various stimuli, the transmission of signals to the motor units and the speed of physical response of the body to these signals.

There are two ways in which response initiation time can be reduced in gymnastics. Although nerves transmit signals at different speeds their individual speeds are constant and cannot be changed, so there are no gains to be effected in this area. However, in gymnastic moves the transmission time of signals represents a small percentage of the response initiation time. The gains are in the areas of processing and analysing the signals and increasing the rate of physical response to the motor signals.

Large gains in response initiation time can be achieved by reducing the processing time. Processing can be considered to exist within a wide band. Spinal reflex which is the fastest form of processing is one extreme. Here the movement in response to the stimuli may have occurred even before the message reaches the brain—withdrawal from heat or pain, and so on. At the other extreme end, the information processing may be slow, e.g. deciding what mark to give for a vault. The secret of reducing response initiation time in gymnastics, is repetition of the skill being learned. The more often the skill is performed, the faster will be the gymnast's response to the situation stimulus.

The second area of gain is to increase the physical response of the body to signals passed to the motor neurons, that is the rate at which the musculoskeletal systems responds. This will obviously depend on the speed of muscular contraction and hence on the strength to weight ratio of the gymnast. We will show later that the acceleration of a body or element of given mass (or weight) is directly related to the force being applied. Hence, everything else being equal, the stronger the muscle providing the motive force, the faster the acceleration of the relevant body parts will be. So strength is an important factor in reducing response initiation time.

Summary

1   A lever is a solid bar which is pivoted at a fixed point known as the fulcrum in such a way that rotation about the fulcrum will occur if a force is applied at a specified point to overcome a weight or resistance.
2   There are three types of levers depending on the relative positions of the fulcrum and point of application of the force and resistance (or weight).
3   The human body is made up of complex arrangements of anatomic levers, and fully to understand the working of the body the coach should be able to classify anatomic levers into the three types. This is important, as the type of lever influences the forces and movements involved, and hence the physical capabilities of the gymnast.
4   Range of movement of joints are influenced by the type of joint and restraining ligaments, muscles, tendons, etc. Exercises to extend the range of movement include gravity, momentum and resistance type. It is important to record mobility progress and this can be done by using goniometers and Flexometers.
5   Strength is the ability of the body to produce a force or forces and depends largely on the number and size of the muscle fibres and the ability to stimulate as many muscle fibres as possible.
6   Exercises for increasing strength can be grouped into three

categories: isotonic, isometric and isokinetic. Again it is important that strength improvements are measured and recorded to help the coach evaluate the usefulness of training programmes, and to encourage the gymnast.

7 There are several methods of assessing strength which include how many (say for chins, etc.), how much (use of weights, dynamometers, etc.), and how fast (timed exercises).

8 Body movement is initiated, monitored and controlled by the neuromuscular system. In gymnastics, it is important that the body is able to respond quickly to stimuli. Reductions in response initiation time can be achieved by repetition to reduce the signal processing time, and by strength increases to increase the speed of muscular contractions and hence increase the speed of body movements.

Revision Questions

1 If press-ups were used as a means of measuring strength improvement in a new gymnast and a graph was plotted of the number of press-ups recorded against time, what would be the expected shape of the graph? Check this in practice and consider the implication for strength training.

2 Consider the implication of response initiation time in spotting. How would this influence you in your own programme of skills learning, or when designing a programme of skills learning for a new coach?

3 How many relevant strength training situations could you create using a bathroom scales as a dynamometer? What steps would you take to ensure the training and tests are carried out under controlled conditions.

4 Why are most anatomical levers inefficient? (I suggest you examine Fig. 1 and relate it to the point of application of a force to close a door.)

2

Centre of Gravity and Stability

The mass of a gymnast is distributed throughout the whole of the body, but it is often convenient to locate and consider the one point within the body at which the whole of the mass of the gymnast can be considered to act. This point is known as the centre of gravity. Put another way, it is the one point at which the body can be supported without any tendency to move, that is the balance point.

The terms 'on balance' and 'off balance' are frequently used in gymnasiums. We can now consider precisely what these mean. A gymnast is in an 'on balance' position when the centre of gravity is directly above the support point or area of support. In this situation there is no tendency for the gymnast to move, that is to say the gymnast is in a relatively stable position. Conversely, when the centre of gravity of the gymnast is not above the area of support, an 'off balance' situation occurs and body movement is inevitable. The gymnast is in an unstable position,

It is convenient here to classify gymnastic moves into two broad categories, *static* and *dynamic*. *Static positions* occur deliberately during exercises to demonstrate balance, strength, flexibility, or a combination of all three. In all static positions the centre of gravity of the gymnast must remain directly over (or directly below for some rings moves) the area of support for the duration of the move. The larger the area of support, the easier it is to maintain balance and hold the desired position. One of the first balance skills acquired by the young gymnast is the headstand. To maintain balance the gymnast must keep the centre of gravity above the area of support. This explains the coaching technique of forming a triangle with head and hands: this provides a large area of support. Provided the gymnast can maintain the centre of gravity above this triangular area, balance is maintained. Within limits, the larger the triangular area of support, the easier it is to maintain balance. For the same reason, it is easier to maintain a handstand on the floor than on the beam, because the area of support is greater (i.e. the centre of gravity can be anywhere, above the two hands on the floor, but must remain above the 10 cm width of the beam); similarly, it is obviously more difficult to hold a one-handed handstand because the gymnast must maintain the centre of gravity above the very small support area afforded by the single hand.

Elegant static moves on the men's rings are the hanging scales, which can be rearways or frontways. These moves demonstrate balance and strength and are of interest because the centre of gravity is below the support (i.e. the rings). Obviously, to maintain these balances the centre of gravity must be immediately below the support. This is shown in Fig. 10 which illustrates the rearways hanging scale. (*Note*: The symbol *G* is used to denote the position of the centre of gravity and *W* the weight of the gymnast.)

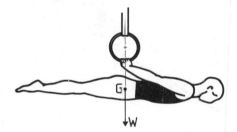

Figure 10 Gymnast in hanging scale rearways on the rings

Dynamic elements are those which require movements of the human body for their execution, and relative movement of one part of the body with respect to another will cause a change in the position of the centre of gravity.

Determination of the centre of gravity for solid inanimate objects is a relatively simple matter. We all know that a ruler will balance in the middle and a circular disc at the disc centre. In studies of human movement the problem is more complex because the body shape and attitude is constantly changing, even during a gymnastic element, and so the position of the centre of gravity relative to the body is constantly changing.

Consider the case of a gymnast in front support position on the bar. As this is an 'on balance' position, the centre of gravity(*G*) must be directly above the bar (Fig. 11). If the gymnast raises the arms above the head as shown in Fig 12, the centre of gravity will move up the body (because the gymnast has redistributed the mass), and will now not be immediately above the support point, that is the bar. The gymnast will have moved from an 'on balance' to an 'off balance' position. Balance has been lost and the gymnast will fall forward.

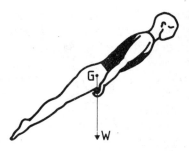

Figure 11 Position of centre of gravity during front rest position

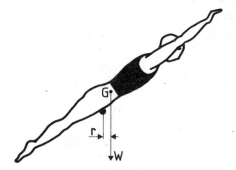

Figure 12 Position of centre of gravity during free front rest position. (*Note*: turning moment = W × r)

This could, of course, be a deliberate action on the part of the gymnast about to perform a free front circle. (This will be discussed in more detail later.)

Situations can arise when the centre of gravity is outside the body itself. This is illustrated in Fig. 13 which shows a gymnast above the bar who has lifted from back support to V-sit prior to a backward seat circle. Clearly here the centre of gravity is in space; it is not within the body of the gymnast. The object of achieving this position is to raise the centre of gravity as high above the bar as possible to facilitate easier execution of the move. The mechanical efficiency of the movement can be improved, by improving the fold of the gymnast, that is by reducing the angle of the V. This will raise the centre of gravity even higher above the bar. A complete fold of legs on to chest would raise the centre of gravity to the highest possible point, and would be a mechanically desirable position. This incorporates the principle of potential which receives fuller treatment later.

Figure 13 Position of centre of gravity during V-sit

From what has been said, it is obvious that the position of the centre of gravity of the gymnast will depend on the body position. It is important for the technical understanding of the execution of a gymnastic move that the coach's eye is trained to recognise approximately where the centre of gravity will be located for different body positions. This is something the coach acquires with experience, especially during spotting. Examples of the position of the centre of gravity for several common gymnastic body shapes are given in Figs. 14 and 15 and these may help in this process of educating the gymnastic eye. It should be noted, however, that the positions of the centre of gravity shown are only approximate, as it depends on the morphology of individual gymnasts. For example, because of the difference in their shapes, the centres of gravity of women are generally lower than that of men. They have more weight distributed around the thighs and buttocks. This difference is important in mature female gymnasts as it will influence the natural timing of their swings on the asymmetric bars and the moments of force involved (see Chapters 3 and 6).

Gymnastic moves can take a gymnast from a position with a large area of support to one with a low support area (that is from a highly stable and safe position to a less stable and less safe position), and vice versa, a typical example being the Stemme or back uprise to handstand on the parallel bars. Figs. 16 and 17 shows that during the swing, when the body is in the vertical position below the bars, the area of support (A) is large (it is that afforded by the contact of the upper arms with the bars). At the completion of the move in the handstand position, the area of support (A) is small, and the centre of gravity must be over the hands. The gymnast has moved through a large to small area of support position, i.e. a position of high

Figure 14 Approximate position of the centre of gravity for different body positions.

Figure 15 Approximate position of the centre of gravity for different body positions (continued)

Figure 16 Back uprise to handstand

Figure 17 Back uprise on the parallel bars

stability to a position of low stability. The position of the centre of gravity relative to the support area is another factor influencing stability (see below).

Gymnastic balances range from those of high stability with a large area of support, which are easy skills for the gymnast to master, to those which have a low area of support and low stability which require great skill to perform. This will be appreciated by studying the balances shown in Figs. 18 and 19, which range from large area of support and highly stable, easy skills, to low area of support, low stability, more difficult balances. Another important factor affecting stability is the height of the centre of gravity above the support. The lower the centre of gravity, the greater will be the stability of the gymnast and hence the balance will normally be easier to hold (all other things being equal). Hence although the area of support is the same for the L support (half lever) as the handstand, the former is a more stable position as the centre of gravity is lower and therefore the balance is easier to maintain. The same argument applies to the forward and Y scales, and partly

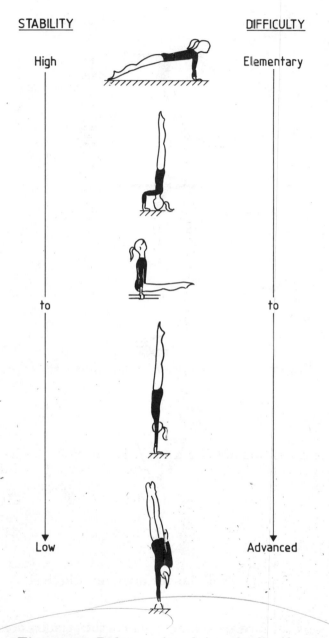

STABILITY

High

to

Low

DIFFICULTY

Elementary

to

Advanced

Figure 18 Balances involving the hands

STABILITY   DIFFICULTY

High   Elementary

to   to

Low   Advanced

Figure 19 Balances involving the feet

explains why the forward scale appears in the primary conditioning set of the National Development Plan for boys, and the Y scale in the more advanced child and youth sets.

A knowledge and awareness of the position of the centre of gravity of the gymnast for different body positions is also important to the coach for spotting. Whenever possible, support should be around and/or under the centre of gravity, whichever is appropriate to the move being supported. For example, support should be around the centre of gravity for cartwheels, under the centre of gravity for forward and backward walkovers, around and under the centre of gravity for flic-flacs, front and back somersaults, around and then under the centre of gravity for a wrap hecht dismount, and so on.

It is important that the supporting effort is being applied to the correct part of the gymnast's body, and in the correct direction. This will become clearer later, after a discussion of force, motion and inertia.

Summary

line of gravity

1 For stability the centre of gravity of the gymnast must be directly over (or in certain cases under) the area of support.
2 The lower the centre of gravity, the greater will be the stability of the gymnast (all other things being equal). However, the act of balancing may be found to be easier if the centre of gravity is higher.
3 Greater stability is obtained if the base of the support is widened.
4 For maximum stability, the centre of gravity of the gymnast should be located over the area of support in such a way that the greatest body movement in any direction can occur without loss of balance.
5 In spotting, support should be around and/or under the centre of gravity of the gymnast.

Revision Questions

1 How would you locate the centre of gravity of one of your gymnasts when the arms are (*a*) at the side and (*b*) stretched above the head? Consider possible coaching implications.
2 Observe gymnastic movements with flight: for example, first and second flight in vaults, free dismounts from the beam, etc. What conclusions can you draw about the flight path of the centre of gravity?
3 What differences would you expect in the relative positions of the centre of gravity of male and female gymnasts? Consider the coaching implications for bar work.
4 Consider the coaching implications for, say, a 360 ° turn on the beam, of the following statement: 'A gymnast has a better balance in motion when he/she focuses the vision on a stationary point.'

5   What path would you expect the centre of gravity of a gymnast to move in when performing shears on the pommel horse?

6   What body position is necessary to raise the centre of gravity of a gymnast to the highest possible position at the commencement of a sole circle on the bar? Why is this, in fact, desirable?

Note: The complete answers to some of the questions will become clearer as the reader proceeds through the book.

3

Force

A force can be defined in simple terms as a push or a pull which will cause or try to cause a change in the motion of the body it is applied to. To determine the effect a force will have on a body, it is necessary to know three things about it:

1   *Its magnitude or size; how large the force is.* There are different units for measuring force, the most common being the newton (N) used in the metric system and the poundal or pound force (lbf) used in the imperial system. Throughout this book, the metric system will be used.

2   *The point at which the force is applied.* This is important because gymnasts are constantly applying forces to gymnastic apparatus and conversely the apparatus is applying forces back to the gymnast. This can be illustrated by considering a simple example of applying a force to a gymnast to prevent him from falling over when he has lost balance. Instinctively the spotter would apply the force at a point high up (A) and not low down (B) the gymnast's body Fig. 20, because he/she is aware that the same force would have a greater restraining effect if applied higher. (Compare this situation with applying a force to open or close a door.) So the point of application as well as the size of the force is important.

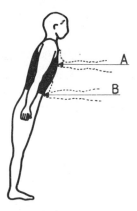

Figure 20 Resisting force applied to prevent gymnast falling over

3   *The direction in which the force is applied to a body.* This is important because it will determine the direction in which the body will move. For example, if a body is being subjected to a single force which is being applied through the centre of gravity of the body, then the body will move in the direction of the force.

As a force must have magnitude (or size) and direction, it can be represented diagramatically by a straight line. The length of the line will represent the size of the force (drawn to scale) and the direction in which the line is drawn will represent the direction in which the force is being applied. For example, if a force of 10 N, is represented by a line 1 mm long, then a force of 20 N, would be represented by a line 2 mm long, a scale of 1 mm representing a force of 10 N.

All quantities that have magnitude and direction can be represented diagrammatically by a straight line and are called *vector quantities*. Hence *momentum* and *velocity* (see below) are also vector quantities and are amenable to graphical analysis.

If several forces act simultaneously on a body, then the one single force that would produce the identical effect to all the forces is know as the *resultant force*. Hence, if we can determine the resultant force, we can ignore the effects of the individual forces. The simplest case would consist of two forces acting in the same direction Fig. 21(a) and (b), or in exactly opposite direction Fig. 21(c) and (d). If both forces act in the same direction, then the resultant force F_R is

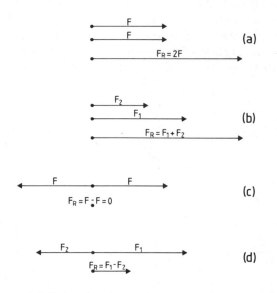

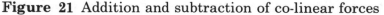

Figure 21 Addition and subtraction of co-linear forces

simply the sum of the two individual forces: i.e. the resultant will be $2F$ in case (a), and $F_R = F_1 + F_2$ in case (b). If, however, both forces act in diametrically opposite directions, then the resultant force will be the difference between the two individual forces, i.e. $F - F = 0$ in case (c) and $F_1 - F_2 = F_R$ in case (d).

The situation is a little more complicated if the two forces are inclined at an angle to one another. In this case, the resultant can be determined graphically (in magnitude and direction), by constructing the *parallelogram of forces*.

(*Note*: Alternatively, for the mathematically inclined reader, the magnitude of the resultant F_R of the two forces F_1 and F_2 inclined at an angle of α can be obtained from:

$$F_R{}^2 = F_1{}^2 + F_2{}^2 + 2F_1 F_2 \cos\alpha$$

inclined at an angle β to F_1, where $\sin\beta = \dfrac{F_2 \sin\alpha}{R}$)

By means of an illustration of how the resultant force can be obtained by constructing a parallelogram of forces, we will consider the chain and wire tensions on the pulleys of the asymmetric bars. Fig. 22 shows the arrangement of the chain and wires commonly found around the pulleys of the asymmetric bars. The pulley is being subjected to three forces as shown. There are two forces F_1 and F_2

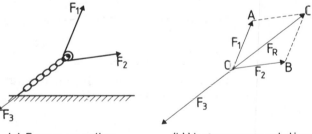

(a) Forces on pulley (b) Vector representation

Figure 22 Parallelogram of forces

exerted by the tension in the wire and a third force F_3 due to the tension in the chain. If we neglect friction in the pulley the tension in the wire on either side of the pulley will be the same $F_1 = F_2$ (action and reaction equal and opposite. (See Chapter 5: Newton's Third Law, page 67.) The resultant of F_1 and F_2 can be obtained by drawing vectors (lines) OA and OB to represent the direction and magnitude of F_1 and F_2 (to scale). Using these two vectors as adjacent sides, a parallelogram can then be constructed. The diagonal of this parallelogram (vector OC) will represent the resultant F_R of F_1 and F_2, in both magnitude and direction. This is the resultant force acting on the pulley due to the wire tension: the resultant is the one single force that will produce the same effect on the pulley as the combined action of the two tensions. This is a very useful tool for the purpose of studying gymnastic moves as the combined effect of two (or more) forces, momentum and so on can be combined to simplify understanding and analysis. It should be noted that all three forces acting on the pulley are balanced (i.e. the pulley does not move). The resultant force F_R must therefore exactly equal the tension in the chain and act in the opposite direction (i.e $F_3 = -F_R$).

Unfortunately, the analysis of most gymnastic moves is a little more complicated. Except for static balances (where the weight of the gymnast acting vertically downwards must balance the vertical components of the apparatus reaction), we are concerned with body movement—that is, we are dealing with a dynamic situation. In this case, it is not technically correct just to consider combining forces. Usually we are concerned with studying the effect on a gymnast of a force (or forces) combined with body momentum of the gymnast. It is, therefore, essential to establish a common base for analysing the combined effect of these different quantities. This can be achieved by considering the *momentum* (or velocity) of the gymnast at an instant in time.

Momentum is a 'quantity of motion' possessed by a moving body and is measured by multiplying the mass of the body m by its velocity v. Hence

$$\text{Momentum} = m \times v$$

This idea is best illustrated by considering an example where a gymnast has momentum, on account of velocity (or speed), and is subjected to a thrust force.

Analysis of the Thrust Phase of a Handspring Vault

Let us consider the thrust phase of a handspring vault. Although as coaches we often glibly talk about this phase of a vault as if it is an instantaneous event, in reality the magnitude of the thrust varies from a value of zero at the start of the thrust phase (initial contact of the hands with the horse) to a maximum value, then reduces again to zero value at the instance of departure from the horse. This is illustrated in Fig. 23(a) and (b), where initial contact with the horse

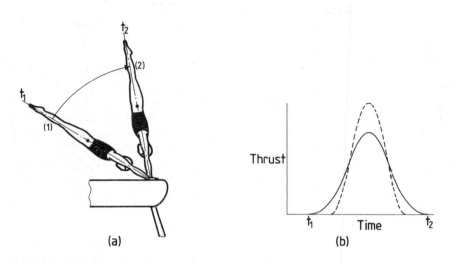

Figure 23 Impulse during vault thrust phase

is at position (1) at time t_1 and departure from the horse is at position (2) at time t_2. An objective of the thrust phase is to reduce the time the gymnast is in contact with the horse $(t_2 - t_1)$ to a minimum, and to maximise the value of the thrust peak (shown by the dotted line). Hence the thrust acts over a period of time (approximately 0.1 to 0.15 seconds), and the magnitude and direction of the thrust varies during this time. The total effect is called the *impulse*, which is the product of the thrust force and the time. The interested reader should see Appendix 2, page 159, for a more detailed consideration.

At the point of impact of hands on horse, the gymnast will possess a linear velocity in the forward direction and hence a linear forward momentum (M_2). The gymnast's body will also have a clockwise angular rotation (and therefore angular momentum), which will be ignored for the moment as it is treated in more detail later (see pages 76–7). The force diagram could be similar to that shown in Fig. 24. The weight of the gymnast W is acting vertically downwards through the centre of gravity, and there is also a thrust force F whose magnitude and direction can change during the thrust phase. The effect of the force F is twofold. First, it will change the speed of rotation of the body if it does not pass through the centre of gravity (see below), and secondly, it will impart an upward momentum to gymnast due to the impulsive effect. This impulsive thrust momentum M_1 will pass through the centre of gravity of the gymnast in a direction parallel to the force F.

If the magnitude of the momentum vectors M_1 and M_2 are known and the lengths of the lines representing them are drawn to scale, then the resultant momentum of the gymnast can be determined by

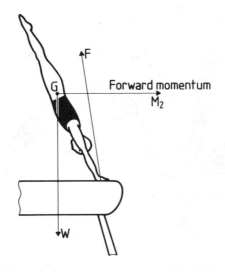

Figure 24 The thrust phase of a handspring vault (*Note*: F need not necessarily act in line with the body.)

constructing a parallelogram. If M_1 and M_2 form adjacent sides of the parallelogram, then the resultant of these two vectors will be represented in magnitude and direction by the diagonal as shown in Fig. 25. This means we can now forget that the gymnast is under the action of two effects, because we know that the centre of gravity will move in the direction of resultant momentum vector M_R. Obviously if there were no other influences acting on the gymnast, he would never again descend to earth. But as gravity acts on the body, the flight path of the second flight (which starts off in the direction of M_R) will be similar to that shown by the broken line. The force of gravity is playing its part in pulling the gymnast down to the landing position.

This is a deliberate over-simplification of a very complex situation. The effects of body changes during the compression and repulsion phase of thrust, and of friction between hands and horse have been ignored. Also the effect of the centrifugal force (see Chapter 5, pages 68–72) generated during pivotal body rotation about the horse during this phase has not been considered. These points will be dealt with in detail in Chapter 8, which is devoted to vaulting.

In practice (without dynamometer measurements) we do not know the values of the momentum vectors $\dot{M}_1$ and M_2, and we are therefore not able to construct the vector parallelogram to determine the magnitude and direction of the resultant. However, the

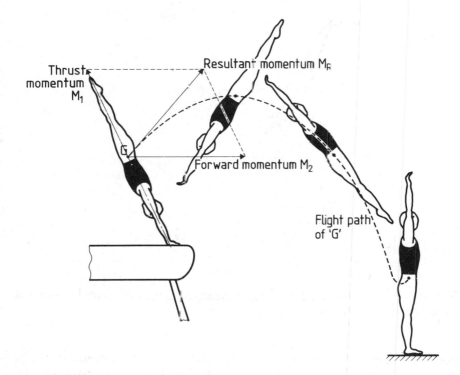

Figure 25 Momentum diagram for handspring vault thrust

concept is useful in identifying the factors contributing to the shape of the second flight trajectory path and to investigate how this can be influenced by technique. This is illustrated in the following example.

Simplified Analysis of the Vault Thrust Phase

It will be demonstrated later that it is impossible to alter the forward momentum (M_2) of the gymnast when he/she is in flight. Hence as the forward momentum of the vault is determined by take-off and cannot be changed after leaving the reuther board the size and direction of the resultant vector M_R can only be influenced by the impulsive thrust applied to the horse by the gymnast. There are three ways in which this can happen to increase the angle of the resultant to the horizontal (θ), and hence increase the height of the second flight.

1 The same impulsive thrust is applied by the gymnast, but it is

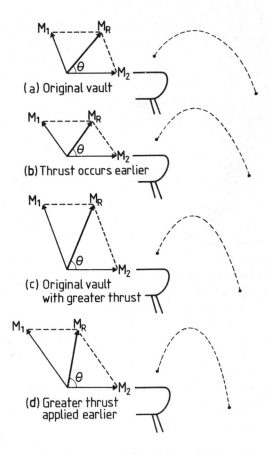

Figure 26 Analysis of vault thrust

applied earlier. This requires a lower first flight and is shown in Fig. 26(b).

2 The first flight trajectory remains the same, but a greater impulsive thrust is applied to the apparatus, Fig. 26(c).

3 A combination of both 1 and 2: greater impulsive thrust applied earlier, Fig. 26(d).

These factors have the effect of changing both the size of the resultant vector and the direction in which it acts, and will produce higher second flights as shown in the diagrams accompanying the parallelograms (Fig. 26). All things being equal this is desirable as it increases the time taken to complete the second flight, and the gymnast will be in the air for a longer time. This means the gymnast will have more time to complete the somersaults and/or twists. (More of this later when we consider flight paths in more detail.)

It will be noted from the flight path diagrams shown in Fig. 26 that as the height of the second flight increases, the length decreases. For an individual gymnast who cannot increase the run up speed and hence M_2 and achieve the maximum thrust of which he/she is capable, then this will always apply. Extra height in the second flight can only be achieved at the expense of distance, and vice versa. This is something the coach should consider carefully as there are deductions for lack of height and lack of distance in second flight in both the Men's and Women's Code of Points.

Flic-Flac Analysis

The flic-flac or back-flip represents a good example of how the application of the principle of a resultant of two factors leads to a better understanding of the technique necessary to perform a gymnastic move. The complete move is shown in Fig. 27, and it can be seen that it is a flight move which requires a 360° rotation of the body. The execution of the movement is largely determined by the

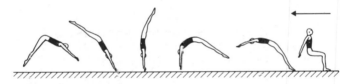

Figure 27 The flic-flac

position of the body immediately before and during take off. As it is a flight move, the direction of movement of the centre of gravity is determined by the take-off position. We will now study this part of the move and show how the identification of the factors involved can lead to a clearer understanding of their effect on execution.

The force diagrams associated with two different body take-off positions could be similar to those shown in Fig. 28. The gymnast's body will have an anticlockwise rotation about the feet (and therefore angular momentum) which we will ignore. (*Note*: The reader will be invited to return to this aspect of the move after turning moments and rotation are considered later in the chapter.) The weight of the gymnast W will act vertically downwards through G and there will be a thrust force F as a reaction to the leg thrust applied to the floor through the gymnast's legs. This thrust F will pass in front of the centre of gravity of the gymnast and will have two effects. It will increase the speed of rotation of the gymnast (see

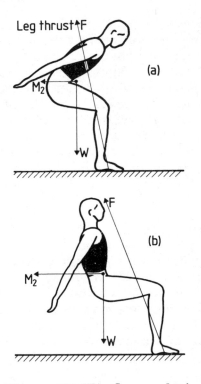

Figure 28 Flic-flac analysis

below), and it will impart an upward momentum M_1 to the gymnast due to the impulsive effect. This momentum vector can be considered to act through the centre of gravity of the gymnast in a direction parallel to the direction of F (i.e. F will help to both elevate and rotate the gymnast).

In addition to the impulsive thrust momentum the gymnast will have a backward momentum M_2 due to the backward movement into the flic-flac. The combined effects of both of these momentum vectors are shown in Fig. 29.

The body position shown in Fig. 29(a) is only just off balance, i.e. the centre of gravity is almost over the point of support (the feet) at take-off. The thrust supplied by the legs will, therefore, be almost vertically upwards. The backward momentum M_2 will invariably be small with this body position as the gymnast cannot be moving backward with any great speed. Hence the resultant will be in a direction similar to that shown, that is near to the vertical. The flight path of the centre of gravity of the gymnast will follow that of the broken line shown, and the result will be a short high flic-flac.

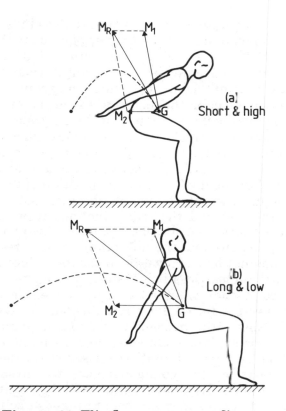

Figure 29 Flic-flac momentum diagram

This is a result which is normally undesirable in floor work where the flic-flac should be low and fast in preparation for another element. However, before simply classifying this as an incorrect starting position for a flic-flac, it should be pointed out that when working young gymnasts in flic-flacs on the beam, the high flight flic-flac produced would provide the gymnast with more time in the air, and hence increase the safety of the move.

The body position shown in Fig. 29(b) is clearly an off-balance one. The centre of gravity is not over the point of support. The backward momentum M_2 would be larger than in the previous case as the gymnast must be moving backwards faster to achieve this body position. The thrust from the legs would be at a shallower angle and so the resultant would be similar to that shown and the flight path of the centre of gravity would follow the broken line. The result would be a faster lower longer move, clearly desirable for tempo flic-flacs.

We should now consider how diagrams such as Figs. 24, 25, 28 and 29 and the accompanying analysis can be of value to the coach. The two moves studied are dynamic in nature, but we have only examined what is happening at one instant in time. However, the position of the body at the instant in time being considered here will have a profound effect on the technical execution of the move. Let us reconsider the flic-flacs. A study of the diagrams will not only enable the coach to appreciate the mechanical forces at work, but also to obtain a visual impression of the expected resulting execution. The coach will be able to anticipate and predict the shape of the resulting flic-flac from the position of the body during take-off. For example, if at take-off the gymnast has the knees in front of the feet and the trunk inclined forward, the coach will predict a short high flic-flac because take-off is near to an on-balance position and the direction of the resultant must be upwards and not back. However, if the lower legs and back are vertical and the upper legs horizontal, this can be recognised as an off-balance position and the resulting momentum will take the gymnast backwards into a long low flic-flac. I have found that diagrams like these are extremely useful teaching aids in the gymnasium, both to explain techniques and to point out faults to gymnasts. I am being continually surprised at the depth of understanding achieved by some young gymnasts, who in some cases, for the first time in their lives, have appreciated the significance of the basic physics principles they are being taught at school.

The ideas presented here will be further developed later in this book, when a variety of gymnastic moves will be studied. However, the reader is encouraged at this stage to take a new look at familiar moves and attempt to identify the mechanical forces involved.

Turning Moments

Whenever body rotation occurs in gymnastics, it can happen in one of two ways.

1 The gymnast may be rotating freely in space: typical examples would include somersaults, free walkovers, free cartwheels and all flight or aerial moves.
2 The gymnast can be rotating about a fixed support point or pivot provided by the gymnastic apparatus: typical examples would include swinging on the parallel bars, asymmetric bars, high bar, and so on.

Some gymnastic moves require a combination of both types of rotation for their execution. For example, in a handspring vault, free body rotation occurs in space about the centre of gravity in the first and second flight phases, but during the support phase the body rotates as a whole about the point of support, which is the vaulting horse itself. This can be seen clearly in Fig. 30. During first flight from position (1) at take off to position (2) when contact with the horse occurs, the gymnast's body has rotated freely in space through an angle of approximately 120°. During the thrust phase, when the hands are in contact with the horse, the body of the gymnast will rotate about the support point, i.e. the hands on the horse. This should be for as short a time as possible. During second flight from position (3) to position (6) at landing, the body is again rotating freely in space about the centre of gravity. Finally, during landing the gymnast will undergo pivot rotation. Rotation occurs about the feet in contact with the floor until the centre of gravity of the gymnast comes to rest above the feet for a perfect landing. (*Note*: This is considered in Chapter 8 on vaulting.)

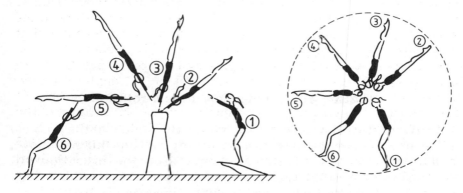

Figure 30 The handspring vault

Free Rotation in Space

If the line of action of a force does not pass through the centre of gravity of a body, it will cause the body to turn or rotate. The product of multiplying the size of the force and the perpendicular (right angle) distance of its line of action (or direction) from the centre of gravity is called the *turning moment*. It is this turning moment or '*torque*' that causes the body to rotate. This is sometimes referred to as eccentric thrust and it is important to realise that the gymnast will rotate in the same direction as the turning moment being applied. If the turning moment being applied to the gymnast is in a clockwise direction, then the gymnast's rotation will also be clockwise; and vice versa.

These points can be illustrated by considering the rotation of the pulley shown in Fig. 31. The pulley is pivoted at its centre of gravity G, and a force of value F is applied to it as shown. The force does not pass through G and hence it has a turning moment effect on the pulley and will cause it to rotate. The value of the turning moment is the product of the force times the perpendicular distance of the direction of the force from the point of rotation G, thus

$$\text{turning moment} = F \times r$$

(where r is the pulley radius).

The turning moment is clockwise in direction and hence the rotation of the pulley will be clockwise.

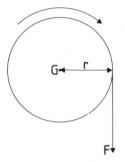

Figure 31 Turning moment and rotation

In gymnastics, however, we are frequently looking at the problem in reverse. We can see the direction of body rotation during a move, and from this we have to deduce the direction of the thrust that will produce the necessary turning moment. Let us examine the body take-off position for a front somersault as shown in Fig. 32(a). This is the reverse lift front somersault. As the gymnast must rotate in a clockwise direction about the centre of gravity to accomplish the move, there must be a clockwise turning moment being applied to the gymnast at take-off, to produce this rotation. This can only happen if the thrust F the gymnast obtains from the floor passes behind the centre of gravity, Fig. 32(b). The turning moment produced will be the product of the thrust F and the perpendicular distance of the direction of F from G (i.e. r).

Therefore turning moment $= F \times r$

The relationship between the value of the turning moment and the speed of body rotation it produces will be examined in more detail later.

Figure 32(b) is an oversimplification of the somersault take-off stage. It assumes that the only force acting on the gymnast is the reactive force F from the floor. The forward or horizontal momen-

(a)
Take off action

(b)
Thrust during take off

(c)
Force components during take off

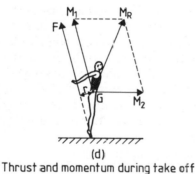

(d)
Thrust and momentum during take off

Figure 32 The front somersault take-off

tum of the gymnast developed by the run up has been deliberately ignored to ensure that the relationship between the turning moment developed by F and the body rotation it initiates is clearly identified.

The reactive force F can be considered as the resultant of two force components: F_1 acting vertically and F_2 horizontally as shown in Fig. 32 (c). Component force F_2 acts in opposition to or 'blocks' the forward horizontal momentum of the gymnast, and depends on friction between the gymnast's feet and the floor. It has the effect of slowing down the horizontal velocity of the gymnast. Component force F_2 provides elevation for the somersault. Hence the resultant effect of F is to provide or increase rotation and convert part of the horizontal momentum of the gymnast into vertical lift.

The situation shown in Fig. 32 (d) is a more accurate representation of the somersault take off. In addition to the thrust momentum M_1, the horizontal momentum of the gymnast M_2 is included. The trajectory and velocity of the centre of gravity of the gymnast at take-off is then determined by the direction and magnitude of the resultant M_R, which is the vector sum of M_1 and M_2 obtained from the parallelogram as shown. It should also be noted that for the somersault shown, elevation and rotation are also assisted by the reverse lift arm action. Rotation has also been assisted by the fact that body rotation about the contact point with the floor, the feet (i.e. pivot rotation), has been initiated during the take-off phase.

At this stage, a re-examination of the thrust phase of the handspring vault and the flic-flac take-off phase (previously discussed, pages 30–8) would be useful. The effect the eccentric thrust has on body rotation can now be identified. In the handspring vault, for the instant in time shown, it is slowing down body rotation (the turning moment is acting in the opposite sense to body rotation, clockwise body rotation, anticlockwise turning moment), whereas for the flic-flac it is helping to increase body rotation, both body rotation and turning moment are anticlockwise in direction.

The reader should now be able to relate front somersault take-off to vault take-off (which is a similar situation), back somersault take-off (which is exactly the opposite in that the direction of the thrust must pass in front of the centre of gravity), and so on.

Rotation about a Point of Support

This can happen in a variety of ways. In the handspring vault previously discussed, the instantaneous point of rotation or pivot during the thrust phase is the point at which the hands are in contact with the horse. In the flic-flac studied earlier, when the gymnast passes through the handstand position body rotation again occurs about the hands which are in contact with the floor. The mechanical similarities of these two moves in terms of body rotation should now be apparent, the only difference being that rotation is forward in the vault and backwards in the flic-flac. Both have free rotation followed by pivot rotation followed by free rotation.

In apparatus work, the apparatus itself is frequently the point of support about which rotation of the gymnast's body occurs. Indeed the gymnast is constantly creating turning moments to produce the necessary body rotation or swinging movements.

Basic swinging, on the parallel bars is shown in Fig. 33(a), and a form of basic swinging, on the side horse, shears, is shown in Fig. 33(b). In both cases, the gymnast has to produce turning moments to intitiate and maintain the swing. This is achieved by displacing the

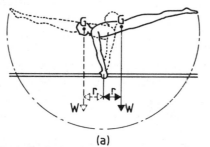

(a)
Turning Moments during Support Swinging on the Parallel Bars

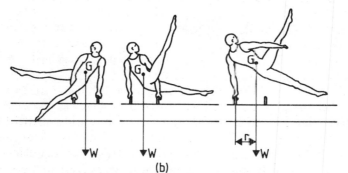

(b)
Turning Moments during Front Shears

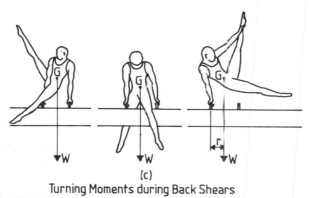

(c)
Turning Moments during Back Shears

Figure 33 Turning moments on parallel bars and side horse

centre of gravity from above the point of support (the bars in the first case and the pommel horse handles in the second case). Again, as the turning moment is given by $W \times r$ its value will obviously vary through the swing, from a maximum at the end of the swing to zero as the centre of gravity passes over the point of support.

Let us now consider the creation of turning moments during bar work.

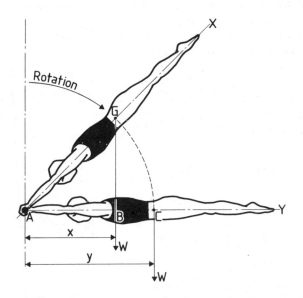

Figure 34 Turning moments during swinging on the bar

Fig. 34 shows a gymnast in two positions during a giant swing on the asymmetric bars or high bar. The direction of the force, i.e. the mass of the gymnast, acts vertically downwards through the centre of gravity due to the pull of gravity. The turning moment in position X is

$$\text{turning moment} = F \times r = W \times AB = W \times X$$

and will be a maximum in position Y when it will be:

$$\text{turning moment} = F \times r = W \times AC = W \times Y$$

Obviously the turning moment is changing throughout the swing, from zero at the top and bottom when the centre of gravity is directly above or below the bar to a maximum in the horizontal position when the perpendicular distance of G from the bar is a maximum.

We will consider later how the magnitude of the turning moment will influence speed of rotation and acceleration.

If we now refer back to Figs. 11 and 12, we can see that raising the arms above the head while in front rest position, displaces the centre of gravity, and produces a turning moment $W \times r$ about the point of support. This turning moment causes the rotation necessary to initiate the free front circle.

A consideration of turning moments leads to a clearer understanding of what is happening during basic swinging on the rings.

'Still rings' is a misnomer. Except during moves designed to illustrate balance and strength the rings are moving. The gymnast is constantly creating turning moments which facilitate the execution of the skill being performed.

Considerable technique and strength is required to achieve horizontal positions on the front and back swing during basic swinging on the rings. When this occurs, there is a large horizontal movement of the rings (up to 1 metre or more, depending on the size of the gymnast (Fig. 35).

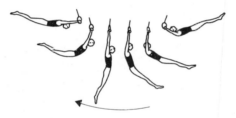

Figure 35 Swinging on the rings

At the bottom of the swing in position A (Fig. 36), the rings and centre of gravity of the gymnast are vertically below the point of support X from the frame. Hence as the gymnast is moving through an on-balance position, the turning moment is zero.

At the end of the back swing, when the rings are in position B, the centre of gravity of the gymnast is still vertically below the support point X. However, the gymnast now has a local point of support the rings themselves, and these have now been displaced from below the wire support point by a horizontal distance r. The gymnast is in an out of balance position and there is, therefore, a turning moment tending to restore him to the equilibrium position A. The value of this turning moment is

turning moment $= W \times r$

A similar situation occurs when the rings are in position C at the end of the forward swing. The turning moment which the gymnast is creating varies from zero in position A up to a maximum of $(W \times r)$ in the horizontal positions B and C at the end of the swings. While this

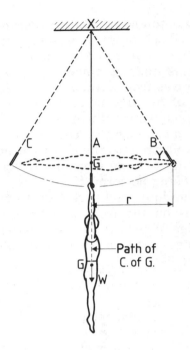

Figure 36 Turning moments during swinging on the rings

is happening the centre of gravity of the gymnast is moving up and down in a vertical direction below the ring frame support point X, as shown (Fig. 36).

The importance of the study of turning moments will become clearer later when we consider their effects on body rotation and inertia.

Summary

1 A force causes (or attempts to cause) linear movement to occur in the body it is applied to.
2 As a force is necessary to cause motion to occur, it is also necessary to stop or prevent movement.
3 If several forces are acting simultaneously, on a gymnast, they can be replaced by a single resultant force which has the same effect.
4 The movement of the gymnast will be in the direction of the resultant force.

5 An eccentric force or turning moment is necessary to cause body rotation to occur and is also necessary to stop or prevent rotation.
6 An eccentric force produces linear movement of the centre of gravity of the gymnast as well as body rotation.

Revision Questions

1 Consider the following gymnastic moves and identify the influences acting on the gymnast during take-off:
   (a) Handspring;
   (b) Free Walkover;
   (c) Front Somersault;
   (d) Back Somersault.
   How can the principle of resolution help to give a clearer understanding of the techniques required for their correct execution?
2 For basic swinging on men's apparatus, e.g. parallel bars, high bar, the gymnast must be constantly creating turning moments about the point at which the swing occurs. How do straight legs and pointed toes help to increase the turning moment generated? (*Note*: Consider the position of the centre of gravity of the gymnast.)
3 The gymnast must be constantly creating turning moments to perform shears on the pommel horse. How does this situation differ from those quoted in the previous question? (*Note*: Consider the point about which swinging occurs.)
4 Why has the emphasis on vault judging changed in the last few years, i.e. emphasis on height and length of second flight? (*Note* the effect the strike angle of the first flight has on second flight trajectory.)

4

Motion

There are certain principles, laws or rules that govern the motion of bodies. These were first completely formalised by Sir Isaac Newton and are incorporated in his equations and laws of motion. An understanding (if only intuitive) of these laws is necessary for an analysis of gymnastic moves. Before developing and considering the application of the equations that govern and predict motion, we must first define some basic terms used in mechanics.

Speed and Velocity

In common use the terms speed and velocity are regarded as having the same meaning. However, in mechanics a distinction must be drawn between the two. Speed is the distance travelled by a body in a given time interval irrespective of the path or direction it is taking. If we say a car is travelling at 50 kilometres per hour we would be referring to the speed of the car, and would consider the direction in which the car is travelling to be unimportant. However, the term velocity means we are not only interested in the rate at which distance is travelled, but also the direction in which the movement is taking place. Hence, to say that a certain gymnast has a velocity of 8 metres per second (m/s) on impact with the reuther board when vaulting is a far more precise statement. It is a statement of how fast the gymnast is running and also indicates that the direction of the motion is also known. This might appear to the reader to be a subtle and perhaps unimportant difference. However, in the analysis of gymnastic moves this distinction is vital. It indicates that velocity, like force and momentum, has magnitude and direction and, therefore, can be represented graphically by a straight line whose length represents the magnitude of the velocity (drawn to scale) and whose direction represents the direction in which movement or motion occurs. The technical name given to quantities such as force, momentum and velocity, which have magnitude and direction, and can be represented graphically by straight lines, is a *vector quantity*.

Acceleration

In common use, the word *acceleration* suggests that a body is moving faster, and conversely *deceleration* means it is slowing down. When a coach shouts at a gymnast to accelerate when running up to vault, it means the coach wants an increase in the run up velocity. Bearing this in mind, we are now in a position to define acceleration (or deceleration) as the rate of increase (or decrease) of velocity.

The most important acceleration in gymnastics is that due to the force of gravity acting on the gymnast. Let us consider the following question. If we drop two gymnasts one heavy and one light, from the gymnasium roof, which one would hit the ground first? Anyone who incorrectly assumes that the answer is the heavy one will be excused, because this is a popular misconception. Both would hit the ground at the same time and with the same velocity. If you still doubt this, I suggest you experiment for yourself (but not with valuable people like gymnasts; a light and a heavy coin will do).

All bodies falling freely under the influence of gravity will accelerate at the same rate of approximately 9.8 metres per second per second (m/s^2). This means that the vertical velocity of falling will increase by 9·8 m/s for each second of free fall. This is very important as every gymnast in free flight will be subjected to this phenomenon.

Resolution

In the previous work on forces and momentum, it was shown how two vectors can be graphically added together using the parallelogram of forces to determine the resultant force. Conversely, a resultant can be broken down into its individual or constituent parts by simply reversing the process. The technique of splitting down a resultant vector into its component parts is known as *resolution of vectors*. Since velocity is a vector quantity it can also be resolved into component parts which, when added together again, will produce the actual velocity of the body. This process is known as *resolution of velocity*. The most convenient way of splitting down a velocity is to resolve it into the two component parts which act vertically and horizontally. The effect of both these parts or components can then be analysed separately, and the final picture obtained by adding the two effects together. Effectively, we have broken down one effect into two separate ones which individually are easier to understand and study.

This is best illustrated by considering a practical situation such as the second flight phase of a handspring vault, shown in Fig. 37. At the commencement of the second flight, i.e. at the point of release from the horse, the centre of gravity G will have a resultant momentum M_R as discussed earlier. The direction in which the centre of gravity moves will be in the direction of this vector (i.e. the resultant dictates the magnitude and direction of the velocity v of the gymnast), which will initially be in the direction of the resultant vector M_R. The velocity v can be broken down or resolved graphically into horizontal and vertical parts v_x and v_y respectively, as shown. To do this, an appropriate scale is selected for v and values of v_x and v_y are then measured directly off the diagram using the same scale. This means that we can determine both the horizontal and vertical velocity of the gymnast at that point, i.e. we know how fast he is moving forward and how fast he is moving upwards. If there were no other influences acting on the gymnast he would continue indefinitely in the direction of the velocity v as a result of the vector M_R. However, as we have stated previously, gymnasts in free flight will be subject to the influence of gravity which is the attraction of the earth's force tending to pull them back to the ground, with the result that the second flight path will be similar to that shown by the broken line. The centre of gravity will reach a maximum height by which time the gymnast has no vertical

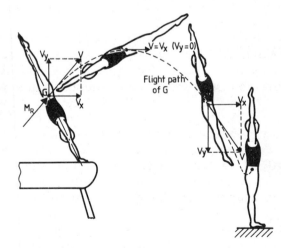

Figure 37 Flight path of centre of gravity and velocity resolution during a handspring vault

velocity (i.e. $v_y = 0$). Therefore, all the velocity v at this point will be horizontally forward. Hence v must equal v_x at this point. From this point on, the gymnast will descend to land under the influence of gravity. The vertical velocity component v_y will increase and reach the maximum value on landing as shown. On landing the centre of gravity has its two component velocities, the horizontal one v_x, which has remained constant throughout the second flight (neglecting the effect of air resistance on the gymnast), and the vertical one v_y which has increased from zero at the highest point of flight to a maximum on landing. The resultant velocity v is a combination of the two component parts. The effect this has on landing technique is considered later when vaulting is discussed in detail.

The path in which the centre of gravity of the gymnast moves (shown by the broken line in Fig. 37) forms a curve which is known as a parabola, and its shape can be calculated precisely in mathematical terms. It is, in fact, the path described by any object propelled or thrown into the air provided we neglect the effect of air resistance on the body. Air resistance on the body, as will be shown later, is a retarding force which tends to reduce the velocity of the body. The flight path of a cricket ball, hit into the air, or a shot propelled by a shot putter, or the centre of gravity of the body of a long or high jumper during the execution of his/her jumps, all follow curves which are parabolic in shape. It can now be realised how important this is in gymnastics, because the path of the centre of gravity of a gymnast in free flight will always be parabolic in shape, and is therefore capable of being studied and analysed, e.g. first and second flight of vaults, all dismounts from apparatus, somersaults, flight out of a handspring, flyspring, headspring, and so on.

There are a set of laws (or rules) that predict the motion of bodies moving in a straight line and enable velocity, acceleration, distance travelled and time taken during a gymnastic move to be determined and related to each other. These are called the equations of linear motion.

Equations of linear motion

These laws can be stated mathematically as follows:

$$v = u + at \tag{1}$$

$$v^2 = u^2 + 2as \tag{2}$$

$$s = ut + \tfrac{1}{2}at^2 \tag{3}$$

where

u = starting velocity of the gymnast
v = final velocity of the gymnast
a = acceleration of the gymnast
s = distance travelled during the move
t = time taken to complete the move

The interested reader can find the derivation of these equations in any basic text on mechanics. These equations for most readers undoubtedly need a little explaining, and we will deal with each equation in turn and then show how they can be used to analyse free flight.

The first equation $v = u + at$ enables the final velocity of the gymnast to be determined if we know the starting velocity, the acceleration of the gymnast and the time taken to complete the move. If we return to the gymnasts we dropped from the gymnasium roof earlier, and decided to note the times taken for both the heavy and the light ones to hit the floor (t), we would be in a position to determine the final velocity (v) with which they would hit the floor (Fig. 38). (Remember, from what was said earlier, that it would be the same in both cases.) Suppose the time taken was 1 second, then $t = 1\,s$, $a = 9.8\,\text{m/s}^2$ (as the gymnast is falling freely under the influence of gravity), $u = 0$ as the starting velocity at the point of release is zero, therefore,

$$v = u + at$$
$$v = 0 + (9.8 \times 1)$$
$$v = 9.8\,\text{m/s}$$

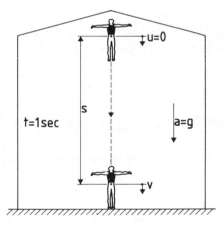

Figure 38 Free fall due to gravity

The gymnast would hit the floor with a velocity of approximately 10 m/s. Obviously we would not have performed this experiment without a good reason. The reason could well be because we wished to know the height of the gymnasium and did not have a tape long enough to measure it. The distance travelled by the gymnast (s) which will be the height of the gymnasium can now be determined from the third equation.

$$s = ut + \tfrac{1}{2}at^2$$
$$s = (0 \times 1) + (\tfrac{1}{2} \times 9.8 \times 1^2)$$
$$s = 5\,\text{m (approximately)}$$

Alternatively, the same result would have been obtained by using the second equation.

$$v^2 = u^2 + 2as$$
$$(10)^2 = 0 + (2 \times 9.8 \times s)$$

i.e. $\qquad\qquad s = 5\text{m (approximately)}$

As a result, this is a little disappointing because we do not have enough height to work high bar safely.

I hope the above example has helped to dispel the fears I know a number of coaches have for anything that is mathematical. Let us now consider how the equations can be applied in a realistic gymnastic situation.

These equations apply only to linear (straight line) motion, and they are not applicable as they stand to gymnastic moves which involve either flight or rotation or a combination of both. However, by resolving motion into horizontal and vertical parts, as discussed earlier, the above equations can be applied to each of the two parts in turn and these can then be put together to produce the whole picture.

Let us now consider the application of these equations to the analysis of a back somersault (Fig. 39). If at the moment of thrust from the ground the centre of gravity of the gymnast is travelling upwards at an angle (θ) of 60° to the ground and, shall we say, with a velocity of 6 m/s, this would represent an explosive take off and a dynamic gymnast. The flight path of the centre of gravity would be parabolic as shown by the broken line in Figs 39 and 40. We first have to resolve the take-off velocity v into its two component parts either graphically as shown in the diagram and discussed earlier, or for the mathematically inclined by the use of trigonometry ($v_y = v \sin\theta$ and $v_x = v \cos\theta$). Either method would give the same results.

$$v_y = \text{upward velocity} = 5\,\text{m/s (approximately)}$$
$$v_x = \text{forward velocity} = 3\,\text{m/s}$$

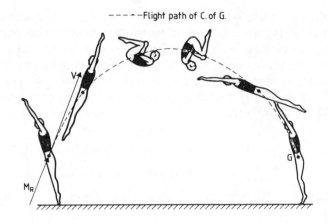

Figure 39 The tuck back somersault

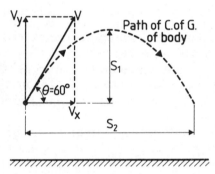

Figure 40 Path of centre of gravity of gymnast during back somersault

The upward and forward movements of the gymnast can now be studied separately.

Consider the upward movement. The initial upward velocity (v_y = 5 m/s) must be the term u. The final upward velocity v at the top of the somersault is zero ($v = 0$). From the point of take off to attaining the highest point of the somersault, the gymnast is decelerating in the vertical direction due to gravity, hence $a = -9.8$ m/s^2 (the negative sign shows the gymnast is decelerating). Therefore,

$t = ?; u = 5\,\text{m/s}; v = 0; a = -10\,\text{m/s}^2$ (approximately)

Using equation (1)

$$v = u + at$$
$$0 = 5 + (-10) \times t$$

Hence $t = 0.5$ seconds

It takes 0.5 seconds to reach the highest point of the somersault and, obviously, 0.5 seconds to descend again to the ground. This means that the gymnast has one second to complete the skill being attempted (somersault, double, full twist, and so on).

Having determined the time taken to reach the highest point, ($t = 0.5$ s), we can now calculate the height s_1 the somersault achieves from equation (2).

$$v^2 = u^2 + 2as$$
$$0^2 = (5)^2 + 2 \times (-10) \times s_1$$

Therefore $\qquad s_1 = 1.25$ m

The centre of gravity of the gymnast rises 1.25 m—a high somersault.

We can now consider the horizontal or backward movement of the somersault. Ignoring the effect of air resistance, the horizontal velocity will remain constant throughout the move, i.e. the horizontal acceleration $a = 0$); Hence the initial horizontal velocity u and the final horizontal velocity v at landing will be the same and equal v_x, i.e. 3 m/s. The horizontal distance travelled during the somersault s_2 can now be determined from equation (3). ($u = v = 3$ m/s; $t = 1$ s; $a = 0$ m/s^2)

$$s_2 = ut + \tfrac{1}{2}at^2$$
$$s_2 = (3 \times 1) + (\tfrac{1}{2} \times 0 \times 1^1)$$
$$s_2 = 3 \text{ m}$$

This means that the horizontal distance travelled is 3 m. This would clearly be a poor tuck somersault—too long in relation to the height.

By varying the angle of the take-off θ, it is now possible by repeating the above analysis to determine the effect the take off angle has on somersault height, somersault length and the time the gymnast is in the air. To be able to directly compare these results, it is essential that the take off velocity is the same in each case, i.e. we are not altering the magnitude of the resultant vector M_R at take-off, simply changing its direction.

The results that varying θ has on a somersault's height, length and time in the air are given in Table 1, and the effects on the flight paths of the centre of gravity are demonstrated in Fig. 41 (page 56).

A study of this table provides some interesting findings. As the angle of take-off θ increases, the somersault will be higher and the move will take longer to accomplish, so the gymnast will have more time available to complete twists, double somersaults, and so on.

HEIGHT = TIME = SAFETY

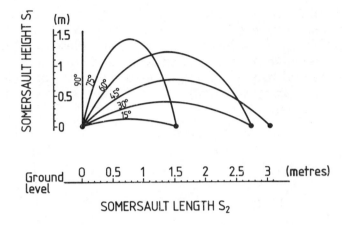

Figure 41 Flight paths of centre of gravity of gymnast for different take-off angles

TABLE 1

Take-off angle θ	Somersault height s_1 (metres)	Somersault length s_2 (metres)	Somersault time to complete (seconds)
15	0.13	1.67	0.29
30	0.41	3.00	0.56
45	0.78	3.33	0.79
60	1.25	3.00	1.00
75	1.47	1.67	1.10
90	1.59	0.00	1.13

In the extreme case, maximum height and hence maximum time can be achieved by a vertical take-off. However, this is not a practical somersaulting position because vertical movement can only be achieved if the resultant vector acts vertically upwards and so there would be little or no turning moment available to initiate the body rotation required to produce the somersault. Hence we have two contradictory conditions. The larger the angle of departure of the flight path from the ground (θ), the more time the gymnast has in the air, but the smaller is the turning moment available to produce rotation. An optimum (or best) angle will exist for a given take-off velocity and move being executed which will be a compromise between these factors.

Although this idea is developed in detail later when the back somersault dismount from the high bar is studied in detail

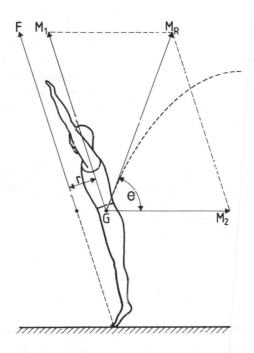

Figure 42 Analysis of back somersault take-off

(pages 126–41), we will now consider the causes responsible for determining the angle of take-off θ of the centre of gravity of the gymnast. Essentially there are two factors acting on the gymnast as shown in Fig. 42. There is a reactive force F from the floor, and also the horizontal backward momentum M_2 generated from the approach to the somersault (i.e. from an arab spring or flic-flac). The reactive thrust F must pass in front of the centre of gravity of the gymnast to produce the clockwise turning moment necessary to increase rotation. As with the front somersault studied previously, the thrust F can be represented by an instantaneous thrust momentum vector M, and a turning moment $F \times r$ (which increases rotation). The velocity and direction of movement of the centre of gravity at take-off is then determined by the magnitude and direction of the resultant M_R, and speed of rotation by the turning moment $F \times r$. It should be noted that this is an oversimplification. Take-off has again been analysed as if it is an instantaneous happening, and the forces involved are constant. This is obviously not the case; body rotation about a pivot (i.e. the feet in contact with the floor) occurs during the rebound stage, and the magnitude of the thrust shown changes during this period. The lifting and rotation effect of the arms during this period have not been included.

The position of the body at departure from the ground merits consideration. Although this angle will obviously vary depending on the strength of the gymnast and the backward velocity of the gymnast into the somersault, body positions of approximately five to the hour are common for gymnasts performing double back somersaults. This is well illustrated in Fig. 43 which shows a gymnast performing a double back somersault tucked.

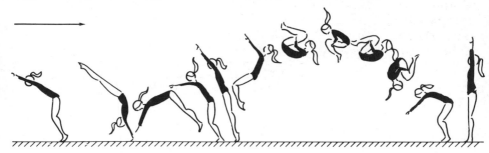

Figure 43 Double back somersault tucked

It is perhaps of interest to note that a take-off angle of 45° will produce the longest somersault (provided the height of the centre of gravity is the same at take-off and landing). This is a fact that has long been known to long jumpers, shot putters, artillery gunners, and others whose objective is to achieve maximum distance. It can also be seen that the horizontal distance travelled (s_2) will be the same for someraults if the angle $\theta_2 = 90 - \theta_1$, i.e. for take-off angles of 60° and 30°, 75° and 15°, and so on.

Although the above analysis has been discussed in terms of a back somersault on the floor, clearly exactly the same principles and analysis could be applied to all aerial or free moves and flight dismounts from the apparatus—e.g. free walkovers, free cartwheels, front somersaults, side somersaults, on the floor; all free dismounts from the beam, barani, front somersaults, back somersaults, twisting back somersaults, double back somersaults; bar dismounts, undershoot, shoot front, backaways, double and triple back somersaults; parallel bar dismounts, back and front out, twisting somersaults and double back somersaults; all rings dismounts; and first and second flights of the vault.

Equations of Angular Rotation

When a body rotates, rotation occurs about a fixed point, or axis, but this will vary in relation to the body, depending on the move being performed, as discussed previously.

To study rotation, the equation of linear motion must be converted to cater for angular motion.

The common measure of angular rotation is the degree. All coaches are aware of the fact that a 360 degree (360°) turn constitutes a full twist. However, in the analysis of rotational movements, the most convenient measure of angular rotation is the radian (rad) rather than the degree. There are 2π radians in a complete turn (where $\pi = \frac{22}{7}$ approximately), hence a radian is approximately 57°. A radian is the angle subtended between two radii when the length of the arc (distance around the circumference) between them is equal to the radius (Fig. 44).

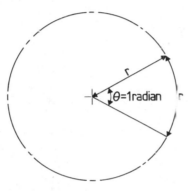

Figure 44 The radian

If ω_1 = initial angular velocity (rad/s) of the gymnast
ω_2 = final angular velocity of the gymnast (rad/s)
t = time taken to complete the rotation (s)
α = angular acceleration (rad/s^2)
θ = angle turned through by the gymnast in accomplishing the move (rad)

then

$$\omega_2 = \omega_1 + \alpha t \qquad (4)$$
$$\omega_2^2 = \omega_1^2 + 2\alpha\theta \qquad (5)$$
$$\theta = \omega_1 t + \tfrac{1}{2}\alpha t^2 \qquad (6)$$

These can be compared directly with equations 1, 2 and 3 (page 51) as they are identical in nature. Unlike linear motion, where the gymnast is being subjected to a constant acceleration due to gravity, angular acceleration is constantly changing during a gymnastic move, and its instantaneous value can only be determined by an analysis of force and energy considerations (which will be dealt with later).

Relationship between Linear and Angular Motion

Let us consider the giant swing on the high or asymmetric bar, (Fig. 45). The gymnast is assumed to start in a handstand position vertically above the bar (AB) with initial angular velocity of zero. Maximum angular velocity ω_{max} will occur at the bottom of the swing (AB$_1$). It will be shown later that this maximum angular velocity ω_{max} will be of the order of 5.5 radians per second at this point. We can now determine the linear velocity v of any part of the

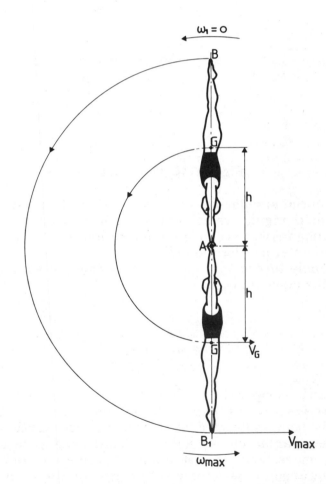

Figure 45 Angular and linear body velocities during a giant swing

body by simply multiplying the angular velocity ω by the distance (h) of the point being considered from the point of rotation.

$$\text{i.e. } v = \omega \times h \tag{7}$$

The centre of gravity of the gymnast will be approximately 1 m away from the bar for a 1.6 m gymnast and so the linear velocity v of the centre of gravity G will be approximately

$$v = \omega_{\text{max}} \times AG = 5.5 \times 1$$
$$v = 5.5 \, \text{m/s}$$

The linear velocity of the fastest moving part of the body v_{max} (i.e. the toes which will be approximately 2 m away from the bar) will be:

$$v_{\text{max}} = \omega_{\text{max}} \times AB_1 = 5.5 \times 2 = 11 \, \text{m/s}$$

Obviously higher values can be achieved with taller gymnasts winding up the swing on the high bar. It should be noted that the linear velocity will be tangential to the arc of rotation at the point being considered. This is important as it is the direction in which the gymnast will travel if release from the apparatus occurs at that point. A tangent to a circle is the direction which is at right angles (90°) to the body line at the point of release, that is, it is the line which just touches the circle and is at right angles to the radius at the point of touching the circle.

We are now in a position to examine gymnastic moves which require flight and rotation for their execution.

Free Cartwheel

Two different take-off positions for a free cartwheel are shown in Fig. 46. Three factors are important in the execution of this move: the thrust from the leg F (and associated momentum M_1), the forward momentum of the gymnast M_2, and the speed of rotation (ω) of the body and leading leg at the point of take-off. A high flight path of the centre of gravity is required to allow the gymnast time to complete the half turn. It should be a short high move (remember our back somersault). This is particularly important on the beam—remember:

HEIGHT = TIME = SAFETY.

For maximum elevation, leg thrust F from the ground should be vertical and pass through the centre of gravity. However, if the thrust passes through the centre of gravity and in a vertical direction then, although maximum elevation will occur, it will not

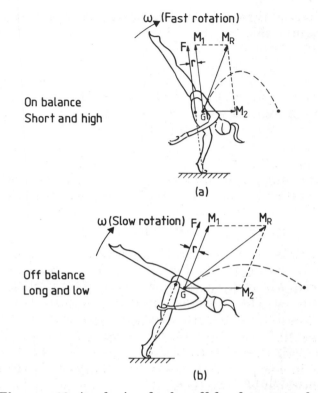

On balance
Short and high

(a)

Off balance
Long and low

(b)

Figure 46 Analysis of take-off for free cartwheel

produce a turning moment which is necessary to increase the body rotation required to complete the move. Therefore, to produce this turning moment the direction of leg thrust must pass behind the centre of gravity of the gymnast as shown in Fig. 46(a).

A study of Fig. 46(a) indicates that a vary fast body rotation (ω) has occurred to allow the leading leg to reach the high position shown, before take-off. The leg thrust is directed approximately vertically upwards acting behind the centre of gravity giving lift and rotation, and the forward momentum M_2 is small showing that the gymnast has simply stepped into the move, and not run into it which is a common mistake with beginners. Hence the take-off position, Fig. 46(a), is mechanically efficient for the execution of the move.

Most of the common faults associated with this move are shown in Fig. 46(b). The angular rotation of the body into the move is slower as the body has not rotated to the required position. The forward momentum is larger, indicating a run into the move. The centre of gravity is well ahead of the thrust leg and the leg thrust F is now directed forward of the vertical. Note the low position of the leading leg and the gap between take-off leg and chest. The result is a long low poor free cartwheel.

From the above example again note:

on balance–SHORT and HIGH

off balance–LONG and LOW

The reader should now be in a position to relate the above analysis to the free walkover. Remember, however, that in this case, extra height and rotation can be obtained by using body action-reaction (what is often referred to as the angry cat-happy cat situation) and the correct lifting arm action similar to the reverse lift (or back up front arm action) used in the front somersault. Body action-reaction will, however, be dealt with later.

Handspring

The handspring is technically more complex than aerial moves because of the extra force involved due to the arm thrust. The take-off position (for a static entry) is similar to that shown in Fig. 47 and the body position and angles are similar to those shown. The objective is again the same, to produce a gymnastic move with high flight. Here, in addition to the thrust F_1 being supplied by the leg (and associated momentum vector M_1) and the forward momentum of the body M_2, there is also a reaction to the arm thrust F_3 against the floor (with associated momentum vector M_3). Hence the gymnast is being subjected to three influences. These influences are all acting simultaneously at a time when body rotation is also

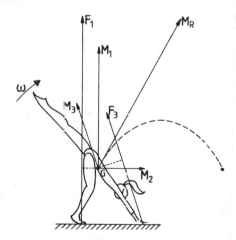

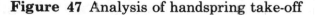

Figure 47 Analysis of handspring take-off

taking place. The magnitude and direction of the resultant momentum vector M_R (a combination of M_1, M_2 and M_3) will govern the direction and velocity of the flight path of the centre of gravity. Hence we need the resultant to be near to the vertical. This can be achieved by:

(a) Increasing the thrust from the leg and ensuring that its direction is as near to the vertical as possible, i.e. get the centre of gravity as near as possible to a position vertically above the thrust leg. A long step into the move is essential here.

(b) Increasing the reaction from the floor, i.e. a more powerful thrust through the gymnast's shoulders and arms. Preparation for good rebound is important.

(c) A lower entry into the handspring; this would mean that the arm/shoulder thrust would occur earlier.

(*Note*: The effects of (b) and (c) can be directly related to the thrust phase of the handspring vault studied earlier.)

It is interesting to note the effects F_1 and F_3 have on body rotation ω. F_1 produces a clockwise turning moment about the centre of gravity and therefore helps body rotation (which is clockwise), whereas F_3 produces an anticlockwise moment about the centre of gravity and therefore slows rotation. This argument only holds true for the instant in time being considered because the magnitude and direction of F_1 and F_3 will be constantly changing throughout the take-off phase.

The above analysis would have to be modified for a handspring performed from a dynamic entry. In this case, maximum leg thrust occurs before maximum thrust is developed through the arms, for a well executed handspring.

Summary

1   The motion of a gymnast under the action of a force (or forces) is predictable and calculable using the equations of motion.
2   For all body movement involving flight, the centre of gravity of the gymnast will move in a predictable parabolic path which cannot be altered after take-off.
3   The horizontal velocity of the centre of gravity of the gymnast will remain constant during a flight move (neglecting air resistance).
4   The vertical velocity of the centre of gravity of the gymnast during a flight move will vary from maximum at take-off and landing to zero at the top of the flight.

5 The angle of take-off, and take-off velocity, determines the time the gymnast will be in the air. Vertical take-off for maximum time, 45° take-off for maximum horizontal distance.
6 On balance take-off positions produce short high flights with maximum time in the air. Off balance take-off positions produce longer lower flight paths of the centre of gravity of the gymnast and less time in the air (all other factors being equal).
7 The rotational motion of a gymnast under the action of a given eccentric force is predictable and calculable using the equations of angular (rotational) motion.

Revision Questions

1 A three-quarter sole circle backwards and underswing (shoot) dismount from the asymmetric bars or high bar starts from a position vertically above the bar, i.e. 12 o'clock. Release from the bar must occur between the half past and quarter to positions, i.e. a rotation of between 180° and 270° before release. Consider the effect varying the release angle will have on the flight path of the centre of gravity of the gymnast and on the time the gymnast is in the air, and hence on the execution of the move. (*Note*: This is treated in greater detail later in the book.)
2 If the gymnast is to perform a skill during the dismount such as a full twist or front somersault, how would this affect the release position?
    (Remember: height = time = safety.)
3 With reference to Fig. 37, it can be seen that the flight path of the centre of gravity is completely determined by the resultant momenentum M_R. Relate this diagram to the discussion on thrust forces in Chapter 3, and consider the effects that the situations given in Fig. 26 would have on the vault second flight in terms of flight time.
4 Why is it desirable to have the hands and head in a straight line when performing a headspring on the floor?

5

Force and Motion

We have already established that a force is necessary to produce body movement, and indicated that if the force is acting through the centre of gravity, then the body will move in a straight line in the direction in which the force is acting. We have also considered the equations of motion that are used to analyse body movement when it occurs. It is now necessary to establish a relationship between force and motion, that is, cause and effect.

The mechanics of certain gymnastic moves are quite complicated as we have already discovered, but the principles which enable us to reduce complex body movements to their simple elemental parts, and so make them more amenable for analysis, are based on three statements known as *Newton's Laws of Motion*. These laws are based on observation, analysis and experiments on solid inanimate objects. The shapes of solid objects do not change and they are not capable of generating forces (action/reaction) within the body themselves. In human movement studies the situation is more complex as the body shape is constantly changing, and the body itself is an energy source capable of producing its own forces internally by muscular movements. However, it is still possible to use Newton's Laws, but care must be taken in their application.

Newton's first law states that: 'a body, if at rest, will stay at rest, or if it is moving with uniform motion in a straight line will continue to do so unless acted upon by an externally applied force.' Conversely, it can be stated that if a body is not being subjected to an externally applied force, it will be either at rest or moving with constant velocity. Put in simple words, a force is necessary to cause body movement to occur, or to cause a change in the velocity of a moving body. The first part of this statement is easy to visualise and understand, 'a force is necessary to produce movement'. The second part of the statement, 'a force is necessary to change the velocity of a body', is less obvious. We expect objects to slow down on their own and eventually to stop without apparently having a force applied to them to cause this to happen. For example, a ball on a snooker table, a car when the driver takes his foot off the accelerator, and so on, will eventually come to rest. However, there are retarding forces and they take the form of friction, through surface contact and air resistance. These are effects which are important in gymnastics and will be considered later.

The first law is of fundamental importance as it is the basis of a formal definition of force as 'the agency responsible for a change in the bodies state of rest or uniform motion in a straight line', i.e. acceleration. This is stated in Newton's second law, that 'the rate of change of momentum is proportional to the applied force'. This can be presented in a different way. 'The rate of change of velocity of a body is proportional to the resultant force acting on it and takes place in the direction in which the force is acting' (provided the body mass remains the same).

Momentum is a 'quantity of motion' possessed by a moving body and is measured by the product of multiplying the mass m by the velocity v.

$$\text{Thus momentum} = m \times v \text{ or } = \frac{W}{g}v*$$

The momentum of a gymnast can only change if the velocity changes because the mass is constant. Hence Newton's second law implies that:

Force = Mass × change in velocity (if mass remains constant).

or Force = Mass × acceleration

i.e. $F = m \times a$ or $= \dfrac{W}{g}a$

(as acceleration is the rate of change of velocity).

The second law tells us that there is a mathematical relationship between the force being applied to a body and the result it causes. The relationship is one of direct proportionality; if the force is doubled, the effect it causes, acceleration, is doubled.

Newton's third law states that 'an action is always accompanied by an equal and opposite reaction'. This is well known to coaches. The harder a gymnast thrusts against the apparatus, the greater will be the reaction of the apparatus on the gymnast.

In the thrust phase of the handspring vault discussed previously, the action of the thrust applied by the gymnast to the horse is balanced by an equal and opposite reaction of the horse on the

* For the mathematically inclined reader this is amplified in Appendix 1 (page 158), where the two systems of force and mass units are presented.

gymnast. From this example, it should be clear that actions and reactions are forces.

In principle, all problems in body mechanics can be analysed by using Newton's three laws. In practice, however, the application may be complex. For example, on the asymmetric bars, in the case of a gymnast laying away from high bar and hip beating the low bar some of the forces involved are unknown and act for a very short time. A further principle based on Newton's first law which simplifies the understanding and analysis of some gymnastic moves involving rotation is the principle of *conservation of momentum*. This states that: 'momentum can only be destroyed by a force and can only be created by the action of forces.' If no external force acts on a gymnast, then his/her momentum remains constant in magnitude and direction.

As most dynamic gymnastic moves involve flight and rotation, we must now consider how the above principles can be applied to angular motion.

Motion in a Circular Path

We have already established the fact that a force applied to a body causes an acceleration, or a change in velocity. However, this acceleration is still present even though the change in velocity is only one of direction. A particularly important case of this type of change of velocity in gymnastics occurs when motion is in a circular path, or under conditions of body rotation.

Consider point A, which is travelling in a circular path of radius r about the centre point O, with constant angular velocity or speed of rotation (ω), Fig. 48(a). The velocity will always be tangential (at right angles) to the path of rotation and will, therefore, be changing in direction. So although its magnitude remains the same, according to Newton's second law, there must be a force present to cause this change in direction of the velocity. Associated with this force, there is a corresponding acceleration. It can be shown that the magnitude of this acceleration due to rotation is:

$$\text{Acceleration} \quad a = \frac{v^2}{r} \quad \text{or} \quad = \omega^2 r$$

It can also be shown that the direction of the acceleration is perpendicular to the direction of the velocity v. It, therefore, acts along the radius towards the centre of the circle O, which is the point about which rotation is occurring. For this reason, it is known as the *centripetal acceleration* (acting towards the centre).

Newton's second law has shown that a force is necessary to

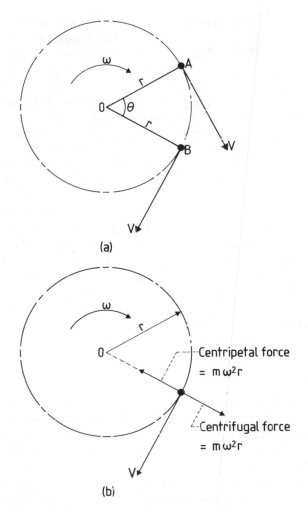

Figure 48 Acceleration and forces due to rotation

produce this acceleration. This force is known as the *centripetal force*.

The magnitude of this force can be determined from the following equation:

centripetal force $= m\omega^2 r$ (absolute units) $= \dfrac{W}{g}\omega^2 r$ (engineer's units)

$$\text{or} \quad = m\dfrac{v^2}{r} \qquad\qquad = \dfrac{W}{g}\dfrac{v^2}{r}$$

when g = acceleration due to gravity
    W = weight of gymnast
v, m, r defined previously

Newton's third law tells us that there must be another force whose magnitude is the same, and whose direction is exactly opposite to this centripetal force (equal and opposite action and reaction). This force is known as the *centrifugal force*, and is present in all gymnastic movements involving rotation.

Several difficult concepts have been presented and these will now be explained through some practical examples.

Everyone who has travelled in a car is aware of the fact that during sharp cornering (even when the speed of the car remains the same) there is a force tending to throw the body outwards, away from the bend. This is the centrifugal or rotational force we have just discussed.

This can be further illustrated by considering swinging a stone round on a length of string, Fig. 48(b). The centrifugal force is the force due to rotation and is tending to release the stone. This is exactly balanced by the tension in the string which prevents release occurring. This is the centripetal or restraining force. Both these forces have the same magnitude and are opposite in direction. The size of these forces are $m\omega^2 r$. This equation can be explained by considering what would happen if the string is replaced by elastic and three simple experiments carried out.

Experiment 1

If the weight of the stone is increased, then for the same speed of rotation the elastic would stretch further. This suggests that the centrifugal force depends on the body weight; in fact, it is a direct proportional relationship. (Double the weight and the centrifugal force doubles.)

Hence if we have two gymnasts of different weight swinging on the bar, with the same maximum angular velocity ω (which will be at the bottom of the swing), then the centrifugal force tending to throw the gymnasts off the bar will be larger for the heavier gymnast. If one gymnast is double the weight of the other, then provided the centre of gravity of both are the same distance from the bar (r), the heavier gymnast would be subject to a centrifugal force double that of the lighter gymnast. (*Note*: It is most unlikely in practice that the centre of gravity would be the same distance from the bar in both cases, but this has been used simply as an example to show that, all other things being equal, the centrifugal force is directly proportional to the weight of the gymnast.)

Experiment 2

If the weight of the stone and the angular velocity was kept the same, but the length of elastic increased, an extra extension would result. This would suggest that the centrifugal force also depends on the length of the string (*r*) or how far away the centre of gravity of the body is away from the point of rotation. Again, it is a directly proportional relationship. (Doubling the distance of the centre of gravity from the point of rotation doubles the centrifugal force.)

Let us return to our gymnasts swinging on the bar. This relationship tells us that the centrifugal force depends not only on the weight, but also on the shape of the gymnast. If we have two gymnasts of the same weight *W* swinging with the same angular velocity *ω*, then the gymnast with the centre of gravity further away from the bar will be subjected to a larger centrifugal force. We can now relate this back to the previous work on centre of gravity. Generally female gymnasts will have their centre of gravity further away from the bar than male gymnasts of the same weight because of the lower distribution of their mass. This would immediately suggest that provided they are swinging through the same angle *θ* (Fig. 49), female gymnasts would be subjected to larger centrifugal

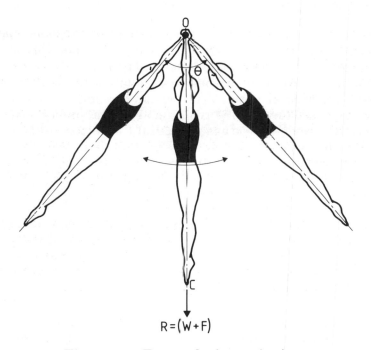

Figure 49 Forces during swinging

forces. (We will show later that this need not necessarily be true because, for a given angle of swing, the maximum angular velocity ω will depend amongst other things, on the distance of the centre of gravity from the point of rotation.) Generally, however, the further away the centre of gravity is from the bar, the slower the gymnast will swing.

Experiment 3

Finally, if the length of elastic and weight of stone remained the same, but the speed of rotation increased, then again the elastic would stretch further. This would suggest that the centrifugal force depends also on the angular velocity. However, this is not a directly proportional relationship. From the previous equation, it can be seen that the centrifugal force is related to the angular velocity squared (ω^2), i.e. if the angular velocity is doubled, then the centrifugal force increases by four times (2×2); if the angular velocity is trebled, the centrifugal force increases by nine times (3×3), and so on.

This means that during swinging on the bar, the larger the swing the larger the maximum angular velocity of the gymnast (at the bottom of the swing), and hence the increase in centrifugal force. The relationship between angle of swing and maximum centrifugal force is considered in detail in the next chapter.

Determination of centrifugal forces is important in gymnastics as it enables us to calculate the forces gymnasts are being subjected to during rotational moves. The centrifugal force (F) tending to throw the gymnast away from the bar will be balanced by an equal and opposite centripetal force which is the tension within the body resisting release (action and reaction are equal and opposite). The centrifugal force F will be a maximum at the bottom of the swing at OC, when the angular velocity ω will be a maximum (Fig. 49). At this point, the gymnast will have to support a total weight of R which will be the sum of the body weight W and the centrifugal force F.

Thus $R = W + F$

It will be shown later that during giant swings, the value of R can exceed five times body weight at the bottom of the swing.

Moment of Inertia

We have already established that a force is necessary to produce linear movement, and a turning moment to produce rotation or a change in angular velocity.

Hence whereas $F = ma$, for linear motion

then $\qquad\qquad T = I\alpha$, for angular motion

Thus a turning moment of value T will produce an angular acceleration α in a body which has a moment of inertia I. (Double the turning moment and we double the angular acceleration of a body if the moment of inertia remains the same.) This is a modification of Newton's second law to produce a mathematical relationship that can be used to explain and analyse rotational movements. However, we have introduced a new term into our vocabulary and this needs defining and explaining.

Stated in simple terms, 'the *moment of inertia* is a measure of how easy or difficult it is to rotate a body', and relates to the term 'lever' which is frequently used in gymnasiums. A long lever would refer to a body attitude with a high resistance to rotation and a large moment of inertia (e.g. straight back somersault), and conversely, a short lever would refer to a body attitude with a low resistance to rotation and a small moment of inertia, (e.g. tuck back somersault).

Although useful for explaining moves to gymnasts, the 'lever' does not have the precision necessary for a study of body rotation. The moment of inertia is essential for this purpose. The moment of inertia I of a body can be calculated from the following equation:

$$I = mk^2 \text{ (or } = \sum md^2 \text{ for body parts)}$$

where k is the radius of gyration of the body and d is body part distances.

We have already met the simplifying concept of centre of gravity as the point at which all the mass of the body may be considered to act. A similar device can be used to explain the meaning of the term *radius of gyration*. During angular motion, there will always be a point about which body rotation occurs. The radius of gyration k is the distance from the point of rotation at which all the mass of the rotating body can be considered to act; hence it also refers to the term 'lever' and is also a measure of how easy or difficult it is to rotate a body. From the above equation, it can be seen that as m, the mass of the gymnast, does not change (at least not during a gymnastic move), then the moment of inertia is proportional to the radius of gyration squared. If the radius of gyration (length of lever) is doubled, then the moment of inertia (reluctance to rotate) increases by four times, and so on. Hence in gymnastic moves involving rotation, the radius of gyration, and consequently the moment of inertia, must be kept as small as possible to reduce the resistance of the body to turning.

Body rotation can occur about any of the three principal body axes. For rotation about these principal body axes (AB longitudinal for twisting moves, EF transverse for front and back somersaults and so on, CD sagittal for side moves, side somersaults and so on), the radii of gyration are shown in Fig. 50. The radius of gyration refers to the radius of the three rings shown. Obviously the greater the radius of gyration the more difficult it is to obtain body rotation.

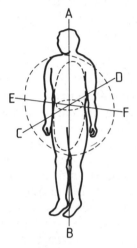

Figure 50 Radii of gyration for principal axes of rotation

The radius of gyration can now be related to turning moment in the following way:

turning moment $T = I\alpha$ (previously stated)

but $I = mk^2$ (also previously stated)

therefore turning moment $T = mk^2\alpha$

As m is a constant (i.e. the mass of the gymnast does not alter), to obtain the same angular acceleration   a greater turning moment will be required if the radius of gyration k and hence the moment of inertia increases. Conversely, if the gymnast reduces the radius of gyration and hence the moment of inertia of the body, a greater angular acceleration will be produced for a given turning moment. Rotation will, therefore, be easier to effect and quicker. Gymnasts and coaches who have never heard of Newton are aware of this phenomenon. Bent legs in, say, a handspring vault, is the young gymnast's subconscious attempt to reduce the moment of inertia of the body (reduce the length of the lever), and hence help to increase the body rotation necessary to complete the move. If this occurs during a vault, it means that the gymnast is not producing a large enough turning moment off the reuther board to rotate the body fast enough in the straight position. The shortening of the body is simply a compensation for this. There are, of course, other reasons for bent legs. Many accomplished gymnasts do this deliberately during warm up, as the vault can be performed with a lower energy input level and is less tiring.

The mechanics of the vault take off is very complex but we will consider a simplification which helps to explain the above statement. To obtain the body rotation necessary for the first flight, the reaction F from the board on the gymnast must at the point of take off pass behind the centre of gravity of the body to produce a clockwise turning moment. This can be seen in Fig. 51. The turning moment is the product of reaction F and the distance of the line of action of F from the centre of gravity, i.e. r.

Thus turning moment $= F \times r = F \times \text{AB}$

Figure 51 Board reaction during vaulting

This turning moment must be great enough to rotate the body quickly enough to put it in the correct position for contact with the horse.

The value of this turning moment can be increased either (a) by increasing the reaction F by jumping on the board harder, or (b) by varying the distance AB either by jumping on to the board at a different angle (so that the line of action of F is changed to that shown dotted), or by changing the body attitude so that the centre of gravity is further ahead of the thrust, or a combination of both.

It should, however, be noted that these changes will also cause not only a change in the rate of rotation of the body, but also in the flight path of the centre of gravity of the gymnast. Refer back to Figs. 24, 25 and 26 on vault second flight and relate this to the take-off phase.

Similar thinking can be applied to the study of moves such as take-off for front and back somersaults where the above are important factors in determining body rotation and flight path during these moves.

Angular Momentum

In the same way as a body moving in a straight line will possess linear momentum, a body rotating about any axis will possess *angular momentum*. The angular momentum is a product of the moment of inertia (I) and the angular velocity (ω). Hence,

$$\text{linear momentum} = \text{mass} \times \text{velocity}$$
$$= mv$$
$$\text{angular momentum} = \text{moment of inertia} \times \text{angular velocity}$$
$$= I\omega$$

These equations directly relate to one another.

Angular momentum can only be created by the action of a turning moment, and can only be destroyed by the action of a resisting turning moment. Therefore, if a body is rotating and is not being acted on by a turning moment (e.g. during flight), the angular momentum remains a constant, i.e. it does not change. Hence during any gymnastic move, if the angular momentum of a gymnast remains constant, a decrease in the moment of inertia (I) will lead to an increase in the speed of rotation and vice versa, i.e. long levers rotate slowly and short levers rotate quickly, all other things being equal.

To initiate body rotation, a turning moment must be applied to the body. The shorter the radius of gyration, the smaller will be the moment of inertia, and body rotation will be easier to initiate and will be quicker. For this reason, it is easier to perform rotational moves in the tuck position than piked, and easier to rotate in the piked position than straight. Simple tests suggest that the ratios of the moments of inertia for these different body attitudes is approximately as follows:

Body attitude	Ratio of moment of inertia
Tight Tuck	1
Pike	2
Straight	4

This means that for a given turning moment the angular accelerations governing the rate of rotation (which vary inversely with the moment of inertia) would be in the following ratio:

Body attitude	Ratio of angular acceleration for given turning moment
Tight Tuck	4
Pike	2
Straight	1

Hence the tighter the body position, the faster will be the rotation and the move easier to execute. This, of course, also explains the 'cowboy' body attitude adopted by gymnasts when performing double and even triple somersaults. The object is to reduce the moment of inertia about the axis of rotation to the smallest possible value and hence maximise speed of rotation.

The principle of conservation of angular momentum can be demonstrated by considering the following gymnastic moves.

Forward Roll

The action of the forward roll is shown in Fig. 52. The move has been shown starting and finishing in the vertical standing position,

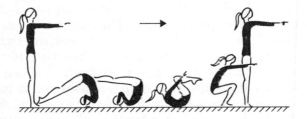

Figure 52 The forward roll

and being executed with bent arms and bent legs. There are of course many variations of the forward roll of which this is one of the simplest. Moving into the roll, the body position is straight with a high moment of inertia and consequently a slow speed of angular rotation. The second position shows that the gymnast has moved forward into a pike position (hence creating a turning moment to initiate the roll, the moment of inertia has been reduced by approximately a half and the speed of rotation increases correspondingly. During positions 3, 4 and 5 the gymnast has adopted a tight tuck position which, in addition to producing the correct ball-shaped body position for rolling, also has the effect of further reducing the moment of inertia with a consequent increase in speed of rotation. The move is completed by the gymnast extending the body from the tight tuck to the straight finishing position shown. During this phase of the move, the moment of inertia increases, the speed of rotation consequently decreases and a controlled finish is achieved.

When analysed from the view point of conservation of angular momentum, there are certain common features between the forward roll and the tuck front somersault, the difference being that during the somersault the rotation is accomplished in the air and not on the ground. To reinforce this important principle further, we will now have a look at the back somersault.

Tuck Back Somersault

As the object of the tuck back somersault is to achieve height, the take off must be near to an on-balance position. The reaction from the floor must be as near to the vertical as possible and pass in front of the centre of gravity to produce the turning moment necessary to increase the body rotation required to complete the move. This aspect of the move was discussed earlier when considering force and turning moments.

During elevation, body rotation is slow because of the straight body position with related high moment of inertia (Fig. 53). During tuck and rotation, the moment of inertia is considerably reduced and the speed of rotation increases. During extension, the body stretches again, increasing the moment of inertia and reducing speed of rotation, making a controlled landing possible. This also applies in reverse to the tuck front somersault. The pike back somersault is more difficult to accomplish because, as the moment of inertia is higher, rotation will be slower and more time is required to complete the move, i.e. greater reactive thrust required at take off. For the same reason, the straight back somersault is a more

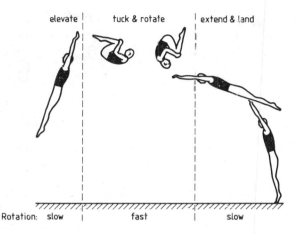

Figure 53 Tuck back somersault

difficult move to execute than the piked somersault.

Side somersaults and moves about the sagittal axis can be explained in the same way. The straight side somersault requires either a larger turning moment and/or greater thrust than a shortened side somersault because of its larger moment of inertia. This makes the move more difficult to perform and gains the appropriate recognition of a 'C' classification in the Men's F.I.G. 1974. Exactly the same reasoning applies to tuck and straight front somersaults.

The same reasoning applies to Tsukahara vaults, where the tuck is easier to perform than the piked, and the piked easier than the straight.

Speed of rotation is important in somersaulting moves performed on the asymmetric bars or high bar. Two examples of somersaults performed on the asymmetric bars are shown in Fig. 54(a) and (b). The first is a somersault forward straddled to catch high bar from an uprise (Janz Roll). The second is a somersault forward to catch high bar from a cast backward from high bar. To perform somersaults of this type, the moment of inertia about the transverse axis (which is the axis of body rotation) is reduced by adopting the straddle fold positions shown. This produces a moment of inertia between that of a tight tuck and a piked position. The wider the straddle and deeper the fold, the smaller will be the moment of inertia., speed of rotation will therefore increase, making the move easier to accomplish. Range of movement is therefore important in these moves.

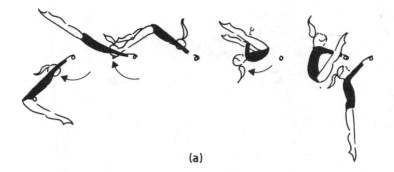

(a)

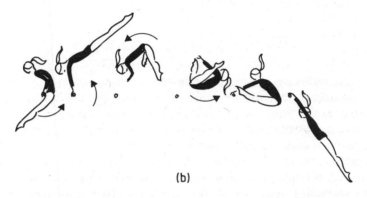

(b)

Figure 54 Somersaults on the asymmetric bars

Rotation about a Fixed Point

In all the above examples, demonstrating the relationship between moment of inertia and speed of rotation, the gymnast was rotating freely in space. We will now consider the coaching implications for gymnastic moves when body rotation occurs about a fixed point.

Fig. 55(a) shows a gymnast swinging freely on the high bar. At the bottom of the swing, the gymnast is in a fully extended position, and the moment of inertia about the point of rotation (the bar) is consequently a maximum. Speed of rotation can be increased by shortening the body and reducing the moment of inertia as shown in Fig. 55(b). This brings the mass of the body in towards the point of rotation and increases the speed of rotation. Obviously the reverse applies. This explains why during circling movements such as giant swings, sole circles, seat circles and so on, the gymnast brings the mass of the body (centre of gravity) in towards the bar during the second half of the circle. This reduces the adverse turning moment

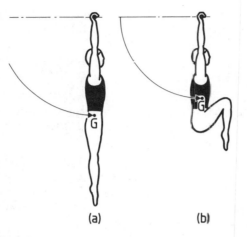

Figure 55 Rotation about the high bar

due to gravity and allows the circle to be completed. This is, of course, only one coaching aspect of these moves. The reader will have a deeper understanding of the mechanics principles governing them after reading the next chapter on energy.

As one final example, let us consider moves related to the family of clear back circles. The timing of the wrist change in the clear back circle is of vital importance. The circle must be completed clear of the bar, with the centre of gravity tracing a path inside the path of movement of the shoulders (Fig. 56). The speed of rotation is

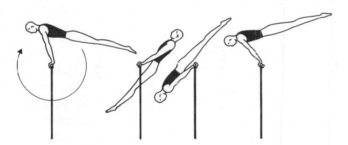

Figure 56 Clear back circle

governed by the distance of the centre of gravity from the bar, i.e. how clear the gymnast is away from the bar. The clearer the circle the slower the rotation, giving the gymnast more time and spatial awareness. This makes the timing and execution of the wrist change easier. Obviously there is a limit to how far clear of the bar the gymnast can rotate, and will amongst other things, depend on the height of the cast backwards from the bar. This again brings in energy considerations which will be dealt with later.

Twisting

We have so far considered body rotation about the sagittal and transverse axes. The same principles apply to rotation about the longitudinal axis for twisting moves.

As the mass of a twisting body is brought in towards the axis of twisting, the speed of rotation increases. Anyone who has watched skaters spinning on the ice is aware of the fact that as the skater brings the arms in towards the body, the speed of rotation increases, and as the arms are extended out again, the speed of rotation decreases. Hence, in twisting moves, the arms can be used as both accelerator and brake. The reason is now obvious. The skater is changing the moment of inertia of the body. This is again an example of the principle of conservation of angular momentum. Reducing the moment of inertia leads to an increase in speed of rotation and vice versa.

This, of course, has important applications to twisting movements and turns in gymnastics. To achieve maximum speed of rotation, the moment of inertia of the body about the longitudinal axis must be reduced to a minimum. To achieve this, a straight body position is required with the arms either kept tight into the body or extended vertically above the head. Note the difference in body atttitudes in Fig. 57. The moment of inertia is a minimum possible in

(a)   (b)   (c)   (d)

Figure 57 Different body shapes

(a), but this position can only be achieved in practice in a narrow range of gymnastic moves largely related to twisting vaults, half on half off, pirouettes on bars and so on. Most twisting moves are performed with the arms in a position similar to that shown in Fig. 57(b). This is the most efficient rotational position possible when it is not possible to have the arms extended above the head.

This body position obviously relates to moves such as twisting back somersaults. The hollow body position shown in Fig. 57(c) is seen all too frequently during twisting moves. It should be noted that a pronounced hollow can increase the moment of inertia about the twisting axis up to two times, and consequently can considerably reduce speed of rotation. Fig. 57(d) shows the worst possible case where, in addition to the arms being extended, there is a pronounced body pike. This can increase the moment of inertia in extreme cases to four times that shown in position (a). Twisting in this attitude is, therefore, not only unaesthetic, but virtually impossible to achieve.

The use of low friction rotating tables to demonstrate these points to gymnasts is highly recommended. Alternatively, rotate gymnasts from a single ring handle and ask them to open and close their legs.

Consider a barani dismount from the beam. Fig. 58(a) shows a body position which is frequently seen in gymnasiums. Not only is it

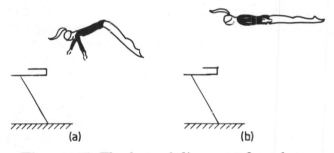

(a)   (b)

Figure 58 The barani dismount from beam

a poor execution of the move being performed, but it makes the next progression (free walkover with full twist) impossible, because it is impossible to achieve another 180° rotation with this body attitude. For correct execution, a straight body position with minimum moment of inertia about the twisting axis is required; see Fig. 58(b).

So a consideration of moment of inertia of the body is often not only important for the move being performed, but also an essential consideration for the next progression.

The full twisting back somersault is shown in Fig. 59. Two 360° body rotations are required for the execution of this move. The gymnast must simultaneously produce a 360° rotation about the transverse (primary) axis (i.e. somersault), and a 360° rotation about the longitudinal (secondary) axis (i.e. a full twist). For maximum efficiency of twisting, the moment of inertia about the twisting axis must be as small as possible, hence the straight body position with the arms wrapped tightly around the chest. A turning moment about the longitudinal axis at take off is necessary to initiate this

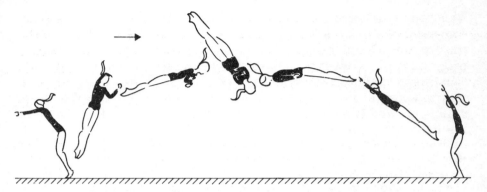

Figure 59 The full twisting back somersault

twist. As the somersault should therefore be accomplished with a straight body position, the moment of inertia about the somersaulting axis, is a maximum, and therefore, a large thrust and turning moment (about the transverse axis) must be generated at take off.

There are a variety of arm actions used in twisting somersaults, but basically the arms should perform three functions. The arms extend above the body during the take off phase to assist the elevation (compare this with the use of the arms to assist lift during standing jumps). The arms should then be wrapped tightly into the body to increase the speed of rotation initiated during take off, i.e. used as accelerators. Finally the arms should extend sideways during the descent stage to slow down the twisting speed and make a controlled landing possible, i.e. used as brakes.

Double and Multiple Twists

Speed of body rotation is increased by reducing the moment of inertia (length of lever) about the rotating axis (and vice versa). To maximise this effect, a maximum reduction in moment of inertia must be produced. This is achieved by setting up initially a long lever rotation and then reducing to short lever rotation (i.e. pulling the body parts in towards the axis of rotation). This was clearly illustrated in Fig. 53 which showed a tuck back somersault. Maximum potential for increase in rotational somersault speed is established during elevation by the complete body stretch shown.

The same principle applies to twisting. Maximum potential for increase in twisting speed can only be achieved if, at the initiation of rotation, the gymnast's body adopts an attitude of maximum moment of inertia (about the twisting axis), consistent with the skill being performed. Let us now apply this thinking to a twisting jump performed from the floor. Maximum moment of inertia about the twisting axis is achieved by stretching the body parts as far away from the longitudinal axis as possible. If we ignore the effect of the legs, this can be achieved by having the arms stretched out sideways (horizontally) from the body. With this body position at take off, maximum potential for increase in twisting speed is established. However, the amount of rotation obtained in a twisting jump depends on four factors:

1   *The height of the jump*—the higher the jump the longer the gymnast is in the air and hence more time is available for rotation.
2   *The initial speed of rotation* (twisting) at take off from the floor. This depends on the magnitude of the turning moment developed between the gymnast's feet and the floor.
3   *The rate of increase in rotation*, which depends on the twisting potential originally established, and the rate at which twisting is increased: i.e. how quickly the body parts can be accelerated in towards the longitudinal axis; this relates to the gymnast's strength ($F = ma$, see below).
4   *The minimum moment of inertia* (about the twisting axis) that the gymnast can finally establish: i.e. how tightly the gymnast can wrap the body parts about the longitudinal axis.

Unfortunately, the factors necessary to establish 1 and 3 are contradictory to one another. Extra time in the air is achieved by vigorously swinging the arms vertically above the head during take off. This technique, however, is in conflict with 3 where the vertical arm swing should stop in the horizontal (sideway) position to set up a long twisting lever to maximize the potential to increase the twisting speed.

Although this situation has not been thoroughly researched by the author, observations suggest that factor 3 has a greater contributory effect to total angle of rotation than factor 1. I suggest you experiment with the following two different arm techniques with a group of gymnasts and measure the rotations obtained.
Technique 1 – Swing arms vigorously upwards above head at the same time as the twist is initiated from the floor. Squeeze arms in tightly to the body.
Technique 2 – Stand with arm extended horizontally (sideways). Originate twist from floor with arms in the extended position. Squeeze arms in tightly to the body.

(*Note*: Allow the gymnasts plenty of time to practise both techniques as one may be more familiar than the other.)

Let us now extend our argument to multiple twisting somersaults. We again face the same dichotomy. To achieve height and hence time in the air to produce twisting, arm swing above the head should be co-ordinated with leg thrust at take-off. This arm action, however, reduces the twisting potential, as to maximise this effect the arms should be extended horizontally (sideways) at the point of take-off. This suggests a compromise arm position at take off where the arms will be swung out sideways at some angle above the horizontal to both assist elevation and set up the potential for rapid acceleration of twisting. The optimum take off arm position will vary from gymnast to gymnast depending on body shape, leg thrust, speed at which arms can be brought into the axis of twisting, and so on. Photographic evidence suggests that for top gymnasts performing multiple twisting somersaults sideways arm elevation of between 10° to 30° above horizontal at take-off are common. This means the emphasis of the arm action is on increasing the potential to accelerate twist rather than assist elevation. It does mean, however, that the gymnast must be capable of producing a straight back somersault with little arm assistance during elevation.

Summary

1 A gymnast, if at rest, will remain at rest or if in motion will continue with uniform speed in a straight line unless acted on by a force.
2 The acceleration of the gymnast is directly proportional to the applied force, i.e. double the force doubles the acceleration.
3 Every action, thrust, force produced by a gymnast must be balanced by an equal and opposite reaction.
4 All rotational movements in gymnastics develop centrifugal forces tending to throw the gymnast away from the point of rotation.
5 When the centrifugal force ceases to act on a gymnast (say at release from the bar while swinging), the centre of gravity will move in a direction tangential to the arc at that point.
6 The momentum of one point of the gymnast's body can be transferred to another point of the body, or to the body as a whole.
7 Speed of rotation (both somersaulting and twisting) can be increased by reducing the radius of gyration and hence the moment of inertia (length of lever). Obviously the reverse also applies.

Revision Questions

1 The height of a swing may be increased by increasing the radius of gyration on the downswing (by extending the body) and shortening the radius of gyration on the upswing. Consider how this principle is applied to the coaching of
   (a) uprises on the high bar or asymmetric bars;
   (b) Giant swings on the high bar with young gymnasts.
2 To maximise the effect of (1) above, the reduction of the moment of inertia (i.e. shortening of the body) should be carried out when the centre of gravity of the body is directly below the bar. Reconsider the moves given above and consider how this provides more detailed information on the timing of when the shortening should occur.
3 Consider how and at what points the gymnast reduces and then increases the radius of gyration of the body when performing forward and backward rolls. Now consider how this would affect the techniques required to perform rolls with bent, and straight legs.
4 Consider how the principle of conservation of angular momentum can lead to a clearer understanding of the techniques involved in
   (a) a Yamashita vault;
   (b) wrap hecht eagle catch on the asymmetric bars. (*Note*: A deeper appreciation of the movement will be obtained after reading the next chapter.)

6

Energy

In common use, the word energy can take a variety of meanings. However, in mechanics its meaning is specific, where energy is defined as 'the capacity of a body to do work'.

The principle of conservation of energy states that, 'Energy cannot be created and it cannot be destroyed, but it can be changed from one form to another.' In the study of gymnastic moves, there are three important forms of energy:

(a) *potential energy*, due to the position or height of the gymnast;
(b) *kinetic energy*, due to the velocity of the gymnast;
(c) *strain or elastic energy*, which can be stored within the gymnast's body or gymnastic apparatus.

Potential Energy

This is the energy gymnasts possess on account of their position or height. The higher the gymnast raises the centre of gravity of the body, the more potential energy is stored. This, for many apparatus moves, represents money in the bank, as the energy can then be used to facilitate the execution of the movement being performed.

The potential energy of a gymnast is measured as the product of the force (mg) in newtons, and the distance the centre of gravity of the gymnast is raised (h) above the equilibrium or datum position in metres (normally height above ground level, or height above apparatus).

Therefore, potential energy $= mgh$
The unit is newton metre (Nm) or joule (J).

This again is a law of direct proportionality. If we double the height (h) we raise the centre of gravity, then we also double the potential energy stored in the body.

Let us now refer to the back somersault discussed in Chapter 4, pages 78–9. The centre of gravity of the gymnast was raised vertically 1·25 m during the execution of the move. If we assume an arbitrary body weight of, say, 60 kg then the work done by the gymnast to raise the centre of gravity vertically by 1·25 m is:

$$\text{Work done} = mgh = 60 \times 10 \times 1{\cdot}75 = 750 \text{ Nm (or J)}$$

Hence at the top of the somersault the potential energy possessed by the gymnast is 750 J. This is the amount of energy stored in the gymnast's body on account of the height.

Obviously the potential energy is changing throughout the somersault, from zero at take off and landing, when vertical velocity is a maximum and $h = 0$, to the maximum of 750 J at the top of the somersault when the vertical velocity is zero and h is a maximum of 1·25 m.

Kinetic Energy

Kinetic energy is the energy possessed by gymnasts on account of their velocity. The faster a gymnast is moving, the more kinetic energy is being stored.

If a body of mass m is moving with a velocity of v, then

$$\text{kinetic energy} = \tfrac{1}{2}mv^2$$

Since the mass m of the gymnast is constant (does not change), then the kinetic energy depends only on the gymnast's velocity v. But we see that this is not a law of direct proportionality. In fact, the kinetic energy depends on v^2, the velocity squared ($v \times v$). That is, if the velocity of the gymnast is doubled, the kinetic energy increases four times (2×2), etc.

Again, referring back to the investigation of the back somersault, vertical take-off velocity (v_y) = 5 m/s. This must also equal the vertical velocity of landing. Hence vertical kinetic energy (at landing and take-off) can be expressed thus:

$$\begin{aligned}
\text{kinetic energy} &= \tfrac{1}{2}mv^2 \\
&= \tfrac{1}{2} \times 60 \times 5^2 \\
&= 750 \text{ J}
\end{aligned}$$

Hence the kinetic energy is a maximum of 750 J at take-off and landing when the vertical velocity is a maximum and the potential energy is zero, and has a value of zero at the top of the somersault when the vertical velocity is zero and the potential energy has a maximum value of 750 J. This is not a coincidence, it merely confirms, the principle of conservation of energy. Throughout the move (considering only the vertical component) the total energy in the gymnast's body is 750 J, kinetic energy being converted into potential energy during elevation (i.e. height increases as velocity decreases), and potential energy being converted back to kinetic energy during the descent stage (velocity increases as height decreases). However, the sum of the two energy forms will always be the same and = 750 J. This principle of equating energy forms is a powerful tool for analysing gymnastic moves as we will demonstrate later.

Strain or Elastic Energy

This is the energy stored in a body due to deformation under the action of a force. A typical example is the energy stored in a reuther board when a gymnast jumps on to it, or the energy stored in the low bar of the asymmetric bars when the gymnast performs a hip beat. The gymnast has to do work on the apparatus to deform or displace it. The kinetic energy of the gymnast (or part of it), is transformed into strain energy which is transmitted to and stored in the apparatus. The strain energy stored in the apparatus is then returned to the gymnast, usually to change the direction and/or the velocity of the body (i.e. as an energy converter); the strain energy is converted back into kinetic energy. We often tell gmnasts to work with and not against the apparatus. What we are really suggesting is that the gymnast learns to time the effort of the move to coincide with the rate at which the apparatus returns the strain energy stored in it back to the gymnast. A simple analogy can be drawn here to illustrate this point, between an uprise on the asymmetric bar and pushing a swing in a park.

Anyone who has pushed a swing in a park is aware of the fact that a considerable swing can be developed with very little effort provided the effort is being applied at the right time. The push must be in sympathy with the natural timing of the swing. The technical name for this is *resonance*, when the timing of the application of the effort exactly coincides with the natural timing (or frequency) of the swing. If the application of the effort is out of phase with the natural timing of the swing, the two effects will work against each other and tend to cancel one another out, and the desired result will not be achieved.

This can now be related to the hip beat back uprise on the asymmetric bars. The gymnast represents the swing and the bar the effort to push the swing. For maximum effective use of the strain energy stored in the bar by the hip beat, the thrust off the bar by the gymnast should coincide with the rate at which the bar returns the strain energy to the gymnast. Both effects should be working in harmony. This is often called *timing*, when the gymnasts are aware of their own natural frequency of swing and the characteristics of the apparatus they are working with, and harmonise the two.

Friction and Heat

In discussing friction in the context of gymnastic movements, it is convenient to differentiate between sliding friction and friction due to air resistance on the body.

In 'sliding' friction, the force which acts equally and in opposite directions along each of the two surfaces in contact eventually reduces their relative motion to zero. Energy can take the form of heat and this is present in gymnastic moves when sliding friction occurs between the gymnast and the apparatus. In bar work, for example, we are faced with a curious dichotomy. The gymnast chalks up deliberately to increase the coefficient of friction between bar and hands and hence reduce the possibility of the hands slipping off the bar. But increasing friction increases the heat generated during swinging and hand tears are more likely to occur. Also as was stated earlier, energy cannot be created or destroyed, therefore, if heat is produced during a move, there must be a loss in useful energy of the move being performed. Hence sliding friction and heat represent a source of energy loss in gymnastics. This means that part of the energy input into the move is simply used to overcome energy losses due to sliding friction and does not contribute to the execution of the movement.

Any body movement of a gymnast is resisted by a retarding force due to its passage through air. This retarding force is known as *frictional air resistance*. The value of the resisting force F_R is given by the following equation:

$$F_R = KAv^2 \text{ (approximately)}$$

where K = a constant depending on the nature of the body surface (e.g. clothes worn, etc.)

A = body area presented to the air resistance

v = velocity of the body

The frictional air resistance is directly proportional to the area of the body and proportional to the velocity squared. Hence at low body velocities, air resistance has a negligible effect on the execution of the move. However, during moves such as giant swings on the high bar, when extreme body velocities can exceed 13 m/s, air resistance can represent a significant resisting force. This again means an energy input into the move is required simply to overcome the air resistance opposing the move.

Energy Conversion

Energy conversion will now be demonstrated by considering selected gymnastic movements. Fig. 60 shows the typical path described by the centre of gravity of a gymnast performing a handspring vault.

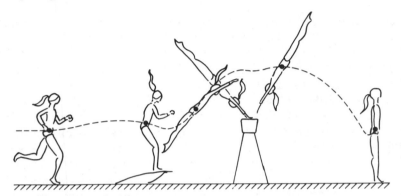

Figure 60 Path of centre of gravity of gymnast during a handspring vault

At the commencement of the run-up, the gymnast has no energy, i.e. the total energy is zero. During the acceleration stage of the run up the kinetic energy increases to a maximum value which is achieved when the run up velocity reaches its maximum value. During the take-off stage, some of the kinetic energy is converted into elastic strain energy when the gymnast performs work in deforming the reuther board. This obviously means that for the total energy to remain constant, this must be accompanied by a reduction in the kinetic energy and hence in horizontal velocity. At take-off or departure from the board, the strain energy stored in the board is returned to the gymnast in such a way as to alter the direction of motion of the gymnast, i.e. the gymnast is propelled upwards by the board and hence has a reduction in forward momentum. During first flight, some of the kinetic energy of the body is changed into potential energy as the gymnast rises above the horse. During repulsion, when the gymnast thrusts against the horse, there is an increase in kinetic energy, and another change in direction of motion occurs, again projecting the gymnast forward and upward. The gymnast continues to lose kinetic energy with a compensating increase in potential energy until the highest point of the second flight is achieved. During descent to the ground, the body loses all of its potential energy which is converted into kinetic energy. On land, all the kinetic energy is absorbed on impact with the ground and the gymnast comes to rest. Good technique is obviously important here, because unless all of the kinetic energy is destroyed, a perfect landing cannot be achieved. Note the use of the knees as shock absorbers to absorb this energy. The position of the body relative to the flight path is important in ensuring that a good landing is achieved. This is discussed in detail in Chapter 8, on vaulting.

The importance of speed of run-up is now evident. The quality of a vault depends partly on the three energy inputs: the kinetic energy achieved during run-up, the energy input during take-off, and the energy imparted in the form of thrust during the repulsion stage. Consider the initial kinetic energy input to the vault). The only quantity the gymnast can vary is the take-off velocity. This means that if the velocity of run-up is doubled, the kinetic energy of the gynmast (i.e. the major energy input to the vault) increases by four times. Table 2 shows the relationship between increase in run-up velocity and approximate increase in kinetic energy.

TABLE 2

Percentage increase in take-off velocity	Approximate percentage increase in kinetic energy
10%	20%
20%	40%
30%	70%
40%	100%
50%	130%
100%	300%

A 10% increase in velocity at take-off produces approximately 20% increase in the kinetic energy input to the vault. All other figures in the table can be interpreted in the same way, and emphasise the gains to be achieved by training in correct running technique.

Pendulum Swinging

The concept of pendulum swinging is very important in mechanics and it has far-reaching implications for apparatus coaching in gymnastics. Having considered forms of energy and energy transfer, we are now in a position to study the factors governing pendulum swinging.

Mechanical Principles

The simplest form of pendulum is that shown in Fig. 61. The bob is suspended from support point X by a string of length l, whose weight is assumed to be negligible compared with that of the bob. Hence the centre of gravity of the pendulum can be assumed to coincide with

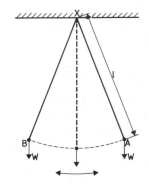

Figure 61 Oscillation of a simple pendulum

the centre of the bob. If the pendulum is given a small displacement, released and allowed to oscillate (swing back and forth) freely, it can be noted that the time taken for each oscillation remains constant, i.e. the time taken to swing from A to B, and back again to A, remains the same for each swing. The time taken for each swing is known as the *periodic time* (T) of the pendulum and is measured in seconds/oscillation, i.e. how many seconds it takes to complete one swing. The value of T (for small oscillations) can be accurately predicted from the equation:

$$T = 2\pi \sqrt{\frac{l}{g}}$$

where π = constant ($\frac{22}{7}$) (approximately)
l = the length of the pendulum
g = acceleration due to gravity

Hence we can see that the periodic time of oscillation of a simple pendulum depends only on the pendulum length. The longer the pendulum, the slower it swings and vice versa. This is not, however, a law of direct proportionality; the periodic time depends on the square root of the pendulum length. This means that if we double the length of the pendulum, the swing slows down; not by a half, but by an amount less than that. For example:

if $l = 0.3\,\text{m}$

$$T = 2\pi\sqrt{\frac{0.3}{10}} = 1.1 \text{ seconds/oscillation (approximately)}$$

and for $l = 0.6\,\text{m}$

$$T = 2\pi\sqrt{\frac{0.6}{10}} = 1.5 \text{ seconds/oscillation (approximately)}$$

Doubling the length does not double the periodic time of swing.

Although we cannot directly relate this simple situation to pendulum swinging on gymnastic apparatus, we can already make the following generalisation. All other things being equal, the longer the pendulum (the taller the gymnast), the slower it (he or she) will swing during suspension (or support) activities. It is important that the coach realises that the timing of pendulum swings in gymnastics is governed by natural laws which relate to the weight and morphology of the gymnast. A gymnast cannot alter the natural timing of a swing without changing the body shape. We will be more precise about this later.

Energy Losses

During pendulum swinging energy losses occur due to friction, as previously discussed. Hence, if a pendulum is displaced to, say, some position A, and released, because of these frictional losses, the pendulum will not return to A, but to some position of lower potential A_1 as shown in Fig. 62. The complete swing can now be explained in mechanical terms.

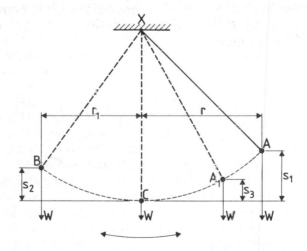

Figure 62 Energy losses during pendulum swinging

The pendulum has been displaced from the vertical position XC to position XA as shown and released. As the centre of gravity has been removed from the vertical, gravity acts on the pendulum tending to restore it to its position of lowest potential. We have created a turning moment of value $W \times r$ and have stored potential energy of $W \times s_1$ in the pendulum. When the pendulum passes through the vertical position, it possesses kinetic energy only, on account of the speed of the swing which is a maximum at this point. (It has lost all its potential energy.) The kinetic energy at this point is equal to the potential energy at the start of the swing minus the frictional losses incurred during swinging from the start position XA to the vertical. After passing the vertical, gravity will again act to produce a turning moment, but this is acting in the opposite direction to the swing and will, therefore, have a braking or decelerating effect. (*Note:* The direction of the swing about X is clockwise, but the turning moment about X ($W \times r_1$) is anticlockwise.) The pendulum will decelerate and finally stop in position XB This is a lower potential position (s_2) than that at the start of the swing. The difference in height between these two points $s_1 - s_2$ represents the loss of potential. This means that the potential energy lost is $W \times (s_1 - s_2)$, and this represents the energy losses due to friction, in swinging from A to B. For the second part of the swing, the pendulum starts with a potential energy of $W \times s_2$ and will reach position A_1 on the return swing. Therefore, the frictional losses during one complete oscillation can be represented as $W(s_1 - s_3)$. Hence the swing of the pendulum will eventually die out altogether unless energy is injected into it. If during the swing there is an energy input of $W(s_1 - s_3)$ to balance out the frictional losses, then the pendulum would return to the start position A. However, if the energy input exceeds the frictional losses then the pendulum would finish in a higher position than it started, i.e. the amplitude of the swing would increase. This principle is important in maintaining and/or increasing pendulum swings in gymnastics. It is important to determine just when these energy inputs should be injected into the swing to have maximum effect and this can be illustrated by considering a model suggested by Hopper (Hopper, 1973) (Fig. 63). The pendulum is released from XA. During the downswing, the length of the pendulum is kept as long as possible to maximise the effect of the gravity turning moment. Hence in the vertical position the maximum transfer of potential energy to kinetic energy has occurred, and the angular velocity will be the maximum it is possible to attain. On the upswing work has to be done to overcome the friction losses if the swing is to be maintained, i.e. the bob must be raised an amount equal to the potential lost ($s_1 - s_3$). This effort should be applied after the bob has passed the vertical position, and

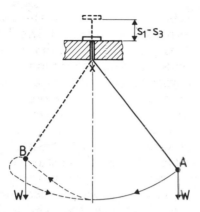

Figure 63 Maintaining the swing by shortening the pendulum on the upswing

will produce the effect shown. The pendulum is lifted to position XB. If the work done in doing this is exactly equal to the frictional losses that occur during one complete swing, then the pendulum will return to the exact starting position XA. This operation can then be repeated indefinitely. If the work done in bringing the mass of the bob in towards the point of suspension exceeds the frictional losses, then the amplitude of the swing will increase.

The angular velocity will be a maximum at the bottom of the swing when all the potential energy has been converted to kinetic energy. Hence the centrifugal force will be a maximum at this point. At the extreme ends of the swing, when the pendulum has a velocity of zero (that is, it is momentarily stationary), there will be no centrifugal force acting and so this is the point at which grip changes, cut catches, and so on should be carried out.

Human Pendulum Swings

Although the study of human pendulum swings is more complex than that of the simple pendulum we have just considered, some of the basic principles governing swinging remain the same. These can be summarised as follows:

1   The height of a swing can be maintained or even increased by extending the body on the downswing (to produce as large a moment of inertia as possible). and by shortening the body on the upswing (reduce the moment of inertia and hence increase the angular velocity).

2   To achieve the above, the centre of gravity of the gymnast

must be brought in towards the point of rotation on the upswing. Muscular effort is required to achieve this and hence work must be done by the gymnast.

3   If the work done by the gymnast in shortening the body (moment of inertia) is equal to the frictional losses occurring during the swing, then the amplitude of the swing remains the same. If, however, the work done exceeds the losses, the amplitude of the swing will increase.

4   To maximise the above effects, the decrease in the moment of inertia (i.e. shortening the swing) should be initiated at the moment the centre of gravity of the gymnast passes through the vertical line of suspension (ie. directly below the suspension point). However, this requires maximum effort from the gymnast (see 5).

5   The angular velocity of the gymnast (speed of swing) will be a maximum when the swing passes through the vertical position and hence the centrifugal force will be a maximum at this point.

6   At the end of the swing, just before its direction reverses the centrifugal force acting on the gymnast is zero. This represents the stationary point during the swing.

In the previous discussion on the simple pendulum, an assumption was made, namely:

'All the mass of the pendulum is located at the centre of the bob.'

This, of course, is not true of a gymnast during suspension or support activities. The mass of the gymnast is distributed throughout the whole of the body and the periodic time of swing on the high bar or asymmetric bars for a small angle of swing is given by the following equation:

$$T = 2\pi \sqrt{\left(\frac{k^2 + h^2}{gh}\right)}$$

where k = radius of gyration about centre of gravity

h = distance of centre of gravity of gymnast from point of suspension

g = acceleration due to gravity

Hence it can be seen that the natural timing of the swing depends on the distance of the centre of gravity of the gymnast, from the bar, and on the moment of inertia of the body about the centre of gravity, i.e. the weight, shape and body attitude. For large angles of swing on the bar, or for basic swinging on the rings, parallel bars or pommel horse, the equations to determine the periodic time are very complex and their treatment is well beyond the scope of this book. However, all forms of swinging are maintained by the creation of turning moments by the gymnast, extending the body on the downswing and shortening on the upswing. Moreover, they are all governed by natural laws as is the case of the simple pendulum.

This means that for any support or suspension swinging activity, the gymnast will have a natural frequency of swing which will be unique for that particular gymnast performing that particular swing. This was referred to briefly under the heading of strain or elastic energy. It is important that the gymnast learns to discover the natural timing associated with different support/suspension swinging activities for different body attitudes. Only in this way can the effort required to maintain or increase the amplitude of swing be produced at the right moment in time.

Pendulum Swinging on the Bar

Basic pendulum swinging on the high bar is illustrated in Fig. 64.

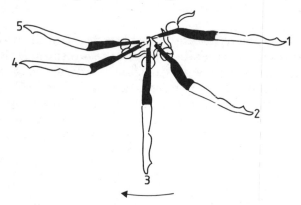

Figure 64 Swinging on a bar

The swing commences in the forward direction from the horizontal position (1). The gravitational moment is a maximum when the gymnast is horizontal and so a straight body position is required to maximise this effect. Prior to reaching the vertical position, the hips lead the legs into the swing (2), i.e. the gymnast is behaving like a double pendulum where the lower half of the body moves relative to the upper half. This has caused a shortening of the body and seems to contradict what was said earlier, that maximum body extension should be achieved throughout the downswing. However, the slightly hollow body position approaching the vertical is then used to set up an action-reaction within the body, and so accelerate the legs through quickly at the bottom of the swing (3) on into the pike required on the upswing (4). At the end of the upswing, the hips are raised, reducing the pike and extending the body (5) to maximise again the effect of the gravitational moment on the reverse downswing.

Basic Swinging on the Pommel Horse

There are two basic types of swinging on the pommel horse, straddle and double leg circles. Straddle swinging has been illustrated in Fig. 33 in Chapter 3, *Force*, and double leg circles in Fig. 65. It has been shown that turning moments are necessary to originate and maintain the swings. We can now appreciate that the turning moments created by the gymnast are responsible for the pendulum swinging that results.

Figure 65 Double leg circle

There is a fundamental difference between straddle swinging and double leg circles. In straddle swinging (even though the gymnast may be performing shears with the legs), the directon of the swing is in line with the length of the horse. In double leg circles, however, the shoulders and head circle in a horizontal plane, and the body swings round in a conical pendulum. These movements, which are illustrated in Fig. 66 and Fig. 67, are simplifications, as the body has been considered as a rigid pendulum.

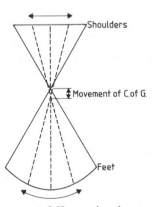

Figure 66 Pendulum straddle swinging on the pommel horse

In both cases, it is essential that the centre of gravity remains reasonably central with the pommel horse handles, the top half of the body being used to counterbalance the legs and hipswing. In straddle swinging and shears the centre of gravity rises and falls and a continuous upward force has to be supplied through the support arms. This teaches and develops strong support.

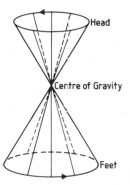

Figure 67 The conical pendulum swing on the pommel horse during double leg circles

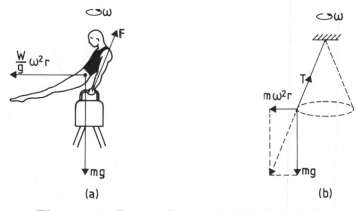

Figure 68 Forces during double leg circles

In double leg circles the centre of gravity of the gymnast does not remain fixed and central as shown in Fig. 67, but in fact rotates slightly. A more accurate representation of what happens is shown in Fig. 68 which shows the forces acting on the gymnast at one instance during the double leg circle. The weight of the gymnast W must act vertically down through the centre of gravity. There is a centrifugal force ($m\omega^2r$) present due to the slight rotational movement of the centre of gravity and there is a thrust F applied to the pommel handles by the gymnast. (*Note*: The direction of F is governed by the grip of the gymnast.) All these forces must be in dynamic equilibrium, i.e. all the forces are balanced. The situation can be compared to that of swinging a weight on the end of a length of string as a conical pendulum which, it can be seen, has similar characteristics; see Fig. 68 (b). (It is called a conical pendulum because of its cone shape.) In this case T is the tension in the string, and again all three forces are balanced. During double leg travels, however, although the height of the centre of gravity above support changes, it will travel along the centre of the horse as the gymnast works along the apparatus.

The motive power for swinging on the pommel horse is similar to that described for high bar in that a large energy input is produced by hip flexion and extension which acts against the support of the arms and shoulder. The hip action should be quick and the change of body attitude small. (To initiate the swing (or angular displacement), moments (or couples) are invariably produced mechanically through the musculoskeletal frame of the gymnast — that is, the centre of gravity of the gymnast is displaced from the original rest position by a muscular effort on the part of the gymnast.) It is the exact timing of the body movement that is the key to success. Again in both these examples the gymnast has a natural swinging frequency which he/she must discover, and then learn to co-ordinate the body action with the natural frequency of swing for the move being performed.

Basic Swinging on the Parallel Bars and Rings

Swinging on the parallel bars can be in upper arm, support or suspension. In all cases, the timing of the swings is governed by natural laws and the statements previously made on pendulum swinging still apply.

Swinging on the rings is a complicated form of pendulum swinging as there are two points of support: local support at the rings themselves, and a distant support, the attachment of the wires to the frame. This was discussed in Chapter 3 (see Figs 35 and 36). Although the pendulum swing is complex, it is important to note that it is still governed by natural laws and gymnasts will have a natural (built-in) timing which will depend on the weight and shape of the gymnast (for fixed apparatus dimension).

It is important that gymnasts experience and recognise the natural timing of basic swings to ensure that the effort or work input is timed to be in sympathy with the natural frequency of the swing. Hence young gymnasts cannot do too much basic swinging.

Energy Conservation and its Application to Circles During Bar Work

Backward seat circle

The word 'potential' was referred to earlier, when we considered the position of the centre of gravity of a gymnast in V-sit above the bar,

(Chapter 2). We are now in a position to be a little more precise in what we mean by the term high potential. At the commencement of a backward seat circle, it is essential that the gymnast stores as much potential energy as possible. To do this, the gymnast must raise the centre of gravity of the body as high above the bar as possible. This can be accomplished in two stages as shown in Fig. 69. The gymnast first lifts from rear rest to a Russian lever 'on-balance' position as shown by the solid figure. The tighter the fold the higher the centre of gravity rises above the bar. The centre of gravity will then be in a position indicated by G. The height of the centre of gravity can be further raised to G_1 by lifting the seat until the gymnast adopts the body attitude shown by the broken line. The gymnast has now achieved the highest possible position of potential consistent with the move being executed. The gymnast is storing the maximum possible amount of potential energy, which is then used in the execution of the movement.

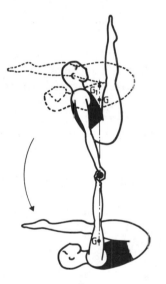

Figure 69 Backward seat circle

After $180°$ of rotation during the seat circle, all the potential energy is converted into kinetic energy (i.e. at the bottom of the swing). As the potential energy lost is a product of the weight of the gymnast (W) and the vertical distance the centre of gravity drops (h), it is obviously desirable to have the centre of gravity as far away from the bar at the bottom of the swing as possible, hence the deep fold in the inverted figure 4 position. If this position is maintained throughout the second half of the move, the gymnast would never complete the circle, as it is impossible to return to the original starting position without an input of energy at least equivalent to the losses of energy that occur during the swing. These losses are due to friction between hand and bar and the effects of air resistance on the gymnast's body. Hence during the second half of the circle, the gymnast brings the seat, and hence the centre of gravity, in towards the bar. This reduces the radius of gyration and hence the moment of inertia about the point of rotation (i.e. the bar), increases the angular velocity and allows the circle to be completed. The finishing position in back support above the bar will have a considerably lower potential than the starting position (i.e. the centre of gravity will be lower). The difference in the two energy levels relects the energy losses that had to be overcome during the circle.

It is suggested that the reader now considers the following moves in the same way: forward seat circles, mill circles, sole circles, clear straddle circles, giant swings.

Giant Swings on the High Bar

The principles of conservation of energy are a powerful tool for studying and analysing circling movements on high bar, asymmetric bars or rings. Let us consider the giant swing (or long swing) on the high bar.

The move is considered to start from a handstand position vertically above the bar (Fig. 70). For maximum potential the handstand should be straight so that the centre of gravity is at the maximum height above the bar. Therefore, maximum potential energy is being stored at the start of the move. On the downswing

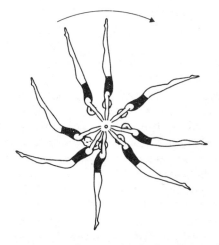

Figure 70 Giant circle backwards

the centre of gravity is kept as far away from the bar as possible to maximise the effect of the gravitational moment. *Note*: The diagram shows just one of many acceptable techniques for performing this move. It can be seen that on the downswing the body is slightly shortened by the pike in the first quarter and the arch in the second quarter of the swing, but will be extended in the quarter past position when the gravitation moment is a maximum.

As the gymnast passes vertically below the bar, the body is shortened by the pike shown. This requires a muscular effort, as the centre of gravity has to be brought towards the bar against the effects of body weight and centrifugal force. To facilitate this, the gymnast approaches the vertical with the hips slightly leading the legs. This aspect of the swing was considered earlier when we studied basic pendulum swinging on the bar (see Fig. 64). To achieve the same high potential position at the finish of the swing (i.e. vertical handstand), work has to be done by the gymnast during the last quarter of the swing to stretch the pike back out to a straight body position. This takes the centre of gravity further away from the bar. This is achieved by the technique of backward rolling to handstand. Thus, there are two energy inputs by the gymnast: shortening the body at the bottom of the swing to bring the centre of gravity nearer to the bar, and stretching the body at the end of the swing to achieve a high potential finish position. To complete the circle, these energy inputs must equal the frictional losses that occur (due to sliding friction of the hands on the bar, and air resistance). If the energy inputs exceed the frictional losses, then the angular velocity of the gymnast will be greater at the completion of the circle than at the start, a feature of dismounts when the gymnast 'winds up' the circles prior to release.

We will now consider how the use of energy conservation can provide coaches with information regarding the magnitude of centrifugal forces involved during the giant swing. The energy method is used, which simply equates the loss in one form of energy to the gain in another, since the total energy in the system must always remain the same.

[*Note*: Readers who do not understand the following analysis should console themselves with the thought that the final derived result is more important than knowing how to prove it.]

At the starting point the gymnast will possess maximum potential energy (Fig. 71) provided the handstand is straight and in the vertical (12 o'clock) position. At the bottom of the swing, in position AB_1, all the available potential energy will be lost and converted into kinetic energy which will be a maximum at that point, when the angular velocity will be a maximum. Hence, applying conservation of energy:

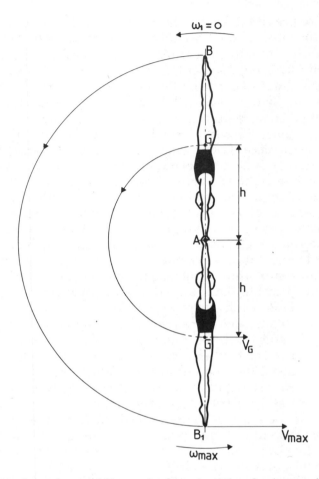

Figure 71 Angular and linear body velocities during a giant swing

Loss of potential energy = Gain in kinetic energy + losses.

The losses, due to friction between hands and bar, and air resistance against the body of the gymnast, are small and will be ignored in the following simplified analysis. Hence the above equation simplifies to:

Loss of potential energy = Gain in kinetic energy

But Loss of potential energy = 2 *mgh*

And Gain in kinetic energy = $\frac{1}{2} mv^2$

$$= \frac{1}{2} m\omega^2 h^2$$

Therefore 2 mgh = $\frac{1}{2} m\omega^2 h^2$

This simplifies to give:

$$4\text{mg} = m\omega^2 h$$

But the centrifual force is given by:

$$\text{centrifugal force} = m\omega^2 h$$
$$\text{or centrifugal force} = 4\,mg$$

Therefore centrifugal force $= 4W$

That is, the centrifugal force acting on the gymnast is a maximum at the bottom of the giant swing and is approximately $4W$ or four times body weight. In addition the gymnast must also support his own body weight W. Hence the total weight F supported by the gymnast is equivalent to $5W$: *five times body weight.*

Therefore it is obvious that a carefully designed training programme providing a gradual progression towards these large centrifugal forces is desirable, especially for young gymnasts. Table 3 shows the relationship between angle of swing θ and equivalent body weight F encountered (Fig. 72).

TABLE 3

Total angle of swing θ	Approximate equivalent body weight F
$0°$	W
$120°$	$2 \times W$
$180°$	$3 \times W$
$240°$	$4 \times W$
$360°$	$5 \times W$

Swings of angle $\theta = 120°$, produces at the bottom of the swing a total force of approximately double body weight. Lay away from the bar to a horizontal position (i.e. $\theta = 180°$) produces an approximate equivalent body weight of three times; a swing of $240°$ achieved by laying away from the bar to a position $30°$ above the horizontal, four times body weight, and the full giant swing five times body weight.

This information may be useful to coaches in designing progressive training programmes.

Forces in excess of five times body weight can be easily achieved in high bar work, especially when a gymnast is winding up the giant swing prior to a dismount when maximum forces of six to seven times body weight can be developed.

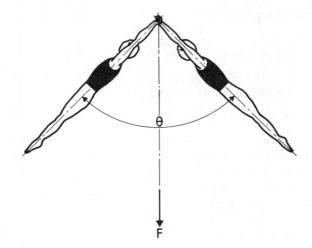

Figure 72 Swinging on the bar

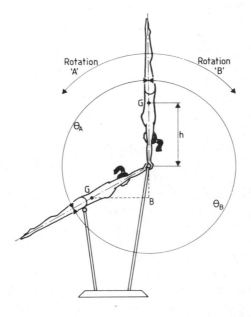

Figure 73 Swinging on the asymmetric bars

Giant Swings on the Asymmetric Bars

The swing is again considered to start from a stationary handstand position above the high bar. The rotation of the swing can be in one of two directions 'A' or 'B' as shown in Fig. 73. The analysis of both situations will now be considered.

ROTATION A

The angle of rotation θ_A will obviously depend on the horizontal spacing of the bars, which itself depends on the gymnast's size. Values for very tall and very short gymnasts have been determined by measurement and are as follows:

Gymnast's Height	θ_A(approx.)
1 7 m	135°
1 2 m	155°

The centrifugal force to which the gymnast is subjected during the swing can be determine by equating the loss of potential energy (i.e. the vertical distance the centre of gravity of the gymnast drops: GB in Fig. 73) to the gain in kinetic energy (related to the increase in angular velocity of the gymnast), as before. Hence:

potential energy lost = kinetic energy gained.

(Again energy losses during the swing are ignored in the analysis.)

$$\text{potential energy lost} = mg \times \text{GB} = mgh\,(1 + \cos(180 - \theta_A))$$
$$= 1.7 \times mg \times h \ (\text{for } \theta_A = 135°)$$
and
$$= 1.9 \times mg \times h \ (\text{for } \theta_A = 155°)$$
$$\text{kinetic energy gained} = \tfrac{1}{2}m\omega^2 h^2$$
$$\text{Hence for } \theta_A = 135°$$
$$1.7\,mgh = \tfrac{1}{2}m\omega^2 h^2$$
Therefore
$$m\omega^2 h = 3.4\,mg$$
Therefore centrifugal force $= m\omega^2 h$
$$= 3{\cdot}4\,mg$$
$$= 3{\cdot}4\ W$$

Similarly for $\theta_A = 155°$, it can be shown that the centrifugal force $= 3.8\ W$

So at the moment immediately before impact with the low bar the gymnast is being subjected to a centrifugal force of approximately 3·4 to 3·8 times body weight. This force is tending to throw the gymnast away from the high bar. In addition the gymnast also has to support her own body weight. Hence the resultant force acting on the gymnast is a combination of these forces as shown in Fig. 74(a).

The resultant force F can be calculated as:

$$F = 4.2\ W \text{ for } \theta_A = 135° \text{ (tall gymnast)}.$$

and $F = 4.7\ W \text{ for } \theta_A = 155° \text{ (short gymnast)}.$

ROTATATION B
A similar analysis can be applied to the swing rotating in direction 'B'. At the moment immediately before impact with the low bar, the

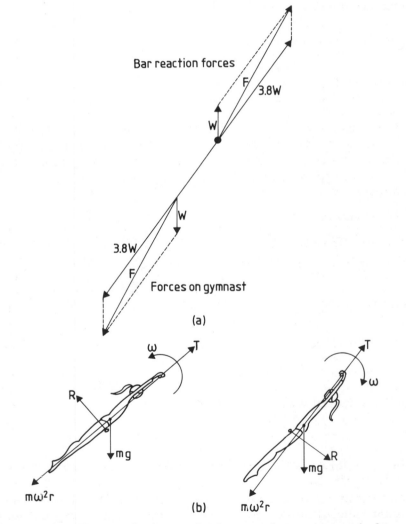

Figure 74 Forces during swinging on the asymmetric bars

forces acting on the gymnast are identical to those for rotation 'A'. The forces acting during impact with the low bar are shown in Fig. 74 (b) for both rotations. However, even larger centrifugal forces are present in the swing. The maximum value of the centrigual force of $4 \times W$ cccurs at the bottom of the swing as shown previously (i.e. total force of $5 \times W$).

From the above analyses, it can be seen that in the extreme condition when the gymnast is at the bottom of the swing, the effective body weight has increased to five times body weight.

On impact with the low bar by swinging from handstand either through direction A or B, the resultant force on the gymnast will be in the range 4.2 to 4.7 times body weight depending on the size of the gymnast. In this case, it must also be remembered that this force is acting on the gymnast at the time when contact occurs with the low bar and this process itself sets up complex force patterns due to the rapid deceleration of the gymnast's body, and the strain energy absorbed in the bar.

It is little wonder, therefore, that during giant swings barstraps can fail, gymnasts can pull muscles or 'fly off' the apparatus, and that even apparatus failure can occur.

It is also interesting to note that during swings in direction A, the smaller the gymnasts (and this usually means younger, weaker and less experienced), the larger the relative forces in terms of body weight they are subjected to, and so the greater the risk of accidents.

Again, what was said earlier on progressive training for gaint swings on the high bar regarding a build-up to these large centrifugal forces is equally applicable here.

In parallel with this, the technique of the move must be mastered and this involves achieving a good handstand position at the commencement of the swing, and correct contact with the low bar at the end of the swing. This aspect of skills training can be achieved and at the same time the forces involved in the move reduced, by adopting the following procedure. Reduce the height of the high bar. The horizontal distance between the bars should be increased to ensure the correct distance for wrapping between the bars is maintained. For a maximum reduction in the forces involved, the bars should be extended to their widest, and the top bar lowered until the correct distance between the bars for wrapping is achieved. This has the effect of reducing angle θ_A which will reduce the maximum force on the gymnast while swinging in direction A. In this way, the whole technique of the move can be practised while the risk is reduced. The bars can then be gradually brought back to the correct settings. This is particularly applicable to small gymnasts where a considerable reduction in the angle of swing θ_A

can be achieved. Coaches could even consider manufacturing an extra long turnbuckle so that the above effect could be fully utilised.

It should be noted that this is not the complete picture. There are other factors to be considered. Although reducing the angle of swing θ_A reduces the maximum force, it will also reduce the time available for the swing. This could be an important consideration when performing, say, the move in the World Set 1981–1984 Asymmetric Bar exercise:

'Facing low bar, cast with legs together to handstand on high bar, pivot 180° to hip beat low bar'

when time available for the half turn is an important consideration.

Back Somersault to Handstand on the Parallel Bars

The back somersault to handstand, or 'flying back' on the parallel bars, is a good example of a gymnastic move which incorporates the principle of energy transfer and conservation of angular momentum (Fig. 75).

Figure 75 Salto backwards to handstand on the parallel bars

A perfectly straight handstand position ensures the gymnast is storing the maximum possible amount of potential energy at the commencement of the move. Obviously the gymnast possesses no angular momentum as rotation has not commenced. During the downswing the body remains straight to ensure that at the bottom of the swing the angular momentum stored by the gymnast is a maximum, and that the gymnast possesses maximum kinetic energy. At the bottom of the swing the gymnast injects energy into the move by kicking in a slight pike. This increases the angular velocity of the legs relative to the trunk in the third quarter of the swing. Release occurs in the horizontal (3 o'clock) position, because the centre of gravity is moving vertically upwards at this point and this ensures that maximum height can be achieved by the gymnast. (Remember the back somersault in Chapter 4; maximum height was achieved when the centre of gravity was moving vertically upwards.) To achieve the stationary handstand at the completion of the move, all angular momentum and kinetic energy must be destroyed by the time the gymnast reaches the vertical position. Obviously the total angular momentum of the gymnast is being reduced during the third and fourth quarter of the swing due to the force of gravity, and kinetic energy is being converted back into potential energy. To ensure a controlled finish to the move, the gymnast varies the relative angular velocities of different parts of the body during the fourth quarter of the move and this has the effect of transferring the ever decreasing angular momentum in towards the final point of support. This is achieved in the following way. Immediately prior to release, the angular rotation of the legs is reduced relative to the trunk. This is characterised by a high hip and chest lift, i.e. the angular momentum of the legs is reduced by transferring some of it to the trunk of the body.

This aspect of the move has been described as the pike/arch or backward leg snap and is shown in Fig. 76. This action provides lift in the fourth quarter in a direction at 90° to the body line (i.e. vertically upwards). Additionally, the leg snap slows the legs down by producing a counter rotation in opposition to the forward swing of the gymnast.

Figure 76 The backward leg snap action

Finally, during the fourth quarter, the angular momentum of the body (trunk and legs) is reduced as this is transferred to the angular momentum of the arms, which rotate very rapidly during this stage. (*Note*: The arms must complete a rotation of almost 360° while the rest of the body rotates through 90°.) In this way, the gymnast has gradually 'killed' the angular momentum of the body. Lastly, the small amount of angular momentum possessed by the trunk is transferred back to the legs, which finally come to rest, due to the retarding influence of gravity, in the vertical position.

It should be noted that the above ignores the range of movement in the shoulder which is an additional feature to be considered in the execution of the move.

Summary

1   Energy cannot be created or destroyed (i.e. the total amount of energy always stays the same provided all forms of energy are considered), but energy is constantly being changed from one form to another in gymnastics.
2   The most important forms of energy in gymnastics are potential (on account of height or position), kinetic (on account of velocity), heat (generated by friction), and strain or elastic (stored within gymnastic equipment due to deformation).
3   Heat generated by friction represents a source of energy loss during a gymnastic move.
4   There is a natural timing associated with pendulum swings on all pieces of gymnastic apparatus. This is known as the periodic time.
5   The height of a pendulum swing or circle on the bar can be maintained by extending the body on the downswing and shortening on the upswing.
6   To maximise the effect of 5, shortening of the body should occur at the bottom of the swing, when the gymnast passes vertically below the point of suspension.
7   At the extreme ends of pendulum swings, the angular velocity will be zero and hence the centrifugal force will be zero.
8   The angular velocity (speed of swing) will be a maximum at the bottom of the swing, when centrifugal forces exceeding four times body weight can be experienced by gymnasts during a giant swing on the bar.

Revision Questions

1   Why does a gymnast have to 'cheat' by bending the legs to perform a complete sole circle which starts from a stationary position on top of the bar?
2   During swinging on the bar, gymnasts carry out grip changes at the end of the swing, i.e. when the swing is being reversed. Consider how this relates to the centrifugal force the gymnast is subjected to at this point.
3   'Great care should be taken with beginners who are swinging on a bar. The hands should be watched for indications of slipping particularly at the bottom of the swing. The safest way for the gymnasts to dismount is to ensure that release occurs at the end of the back swing.' How do these statements relate to the centrifugal force involved?

4 Bar dismounts should be timed so that release by the gymnast occurs at a point where the tangent of the arc at release coincides with the desired initial direction of flight path. Consider the application of this statement to the coaching of a backward salto or forward salto dismount from the asymmetric bars or high bar.

(*Note*: This is treated in some depth in the next chapter.)

5 Consider when release from the bar should occur during a straddle cut and catch. Again try to relate the point of release to the direction of the flight path of the centre of gravity, the centrifugal force, and the characteristics required in the ex- execution of the move.

7

Biomechanics Studies

Biomechanics studies in gymnastics can be divided into two broad classifications: *practical experimentation* and *theoretical analysis*. For a complete and thorough study of a gymnastic move, both approaches should be used. In theoretical analysis, certain simplifying assumptions must always be made to facilitate the calculations involved. Hence the theoretical approach is never a completely accurate representation of the move being studied. (See assumptions made during analysis of the backward salto (backaway) dismount from the high bar, later in this chapter.) However, provided the assumptions made have only a small effect, then theoretical analyses are always extremely useful in providing a basis of understanding of the factors that are necessary for the successful completion of the move. Ideally theoretical analysis should be supplemented by practical investigation, so that the validity of the assumptions made in the theoretical study can be tested. This enables the theoretical results to be modified in the light of what is seen to happen through observation.

Practical Investigations

Practical investigations are concerned with recording what actually happens and then studying and analysing the recorded observations. Mechanics involves the study of *causes* (forces and turning moments) of human movement, and the *effects* they produce (body movement, including flight, rotation, and so on). Hence practical investigation should be capable of measuring and recording both cause and effect.

Dynamometers

Forces and turning moments provide the motive cause for gymnastic moves and these can be measured using dynamometers or load platforms. As was stated earlier a dynamometer is simply a device designed to measure a force or turning moment. The most simple example of a dynamometer is a bathroom scale (previously discussed, page 11) which is designed to measure the force (weight of person) acting vertically down on it.

Dynamometers have been designed which are capable of measuring vertical and horizontal forces and turning moments simultaneously. However, it would not be feasible for the experimenter visually to note three readings simultaneously. Hence, if a dynamometer is being used to measure the causes at take-off for, say, a twisting back somersault which involves horizontal and vertical force components and a turning moment then, for a detailed analysis of what happens at take-off, the dynamometers should be linked to a pen recorder which will provide a permanent record of the forces involved. This is important because the forces involved are not instantaneous but vary in magnitude and direction during the time the gymnast's feet are in contact with the floor (dynamometer) during take-off. (Remember what was said previously about impulses.) In this way, the analyst is able to study the results obtained in great detail and relate them to the effects produced.

Photographic Techniques

The main tools available for studying effect (body movement) are video cameras and cinematographic means.

VIDEO SYSTEMS

Video systems are useful coaching aids, for the execution of gymnastic moves can be captured on video tape and replayed at varying speeds. This provides a very useful diagnostic aid for the coach, because a move can be broken down and studied a frame at a time, and faults easily detected. It also proves useful in demonstrating to gymnasts faults they are not prepared to accept they have. How many times do we hear gymnasts say, 'But my legs were straight.' The camera never lies. For studying moves with twisting elements, two cameras can be used simultaneously. For example, one camera can be recording the somersault, sideways on, and a second camera the twist, head on or from above. With a split screen facility, the move shown from two different angles can be replayed at the same time using half the screen for each. Although extremely useful in the gymnasium as a coaching aid, video is not suitable for detailed studies where an accurate breakdown of the move is required.

CINEMATOGRAPHIC METHODS

Cinematographic methods are widely used to record body movement in gymnastics. Movie cameras with variable shutter speed and adequate illumination are essential. The choice of shutter speed used will obviously depend on the move, or part of the move, being studied. A giant swing on the rings that required approximately two seconds to complete, could well be accurately recorded at 16 frames per second giving 32 shots for the circle. However, a considerably faster shutter speed would be required to investigate take-off during vaulting when the gymnast is only in contact with the board for approximately 0.1 to 0.2 seconds.

A film of the move having been obtained, it can then be studied frame by frame and the results of successive shots laid on top of each other. In this way, a picture of the whole move can be built up and body movements, velocities, accelerations, and so on can be studied.

The results obtained from the analysis of two different glide kips (float upstarts) are shown in Fig. 77. The paths of movement of three parts of the body (the head, hips and feet) have been obtained from a frame by frame analysis of the moves. These have been overlaid on one diagram to give a clear visual picture which enables the coach to study the movement of different parts of the body at any specified point during the move.

The illustrations show two types of float upstart that are currently being executed , and enables direct comparisons to be drawn. For upstart Type 1, the maximum hip extension of 180° occurs at position 5. In upstart Type 2, a maximum extension of 210° occurs at 6 (about 0.15 seconds later than in the previous case), when the hips are thrust vigorously upwards. The effects this has can be seen from the hip and feet glide paths. The work done in raising the centre of gravity for Type 2 (5 to 6) has immediately been lost as the hips drop again (6 to 7). During the stage when the hips are being raised rapidly there is an uneven foot movement. Hence in terms of mechanical requirements only, it may be suggested that upstart Type 2 is less efficient than Type 1. However, the accompanying hyperextension of the body produced can facilitate the kip action, and has aesthetic appeal for some judges and coaches.

Another advantage practical investigations have over theoretical analysis is that by using photographic analysis the effects of body action/reaction can be studied and their effects on the execution of the move determined. This can then be used to supplement and/or modify the results of the theoretical studies. This would be of particular significance in, say, a handspring front somersault vault where a low hollow body first flight is frequently used to provide a considerable body action/reaction to facilitate the execution of the somersault.

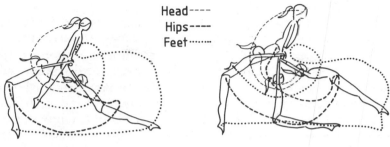

Type 1   Type 2

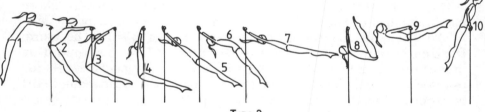

Type 1

Type 2

Figure 77 Photographic comparison of two glide kips (float upstarts)

ChronocyclegraphicStudies

Chronocyclegraphic photography is a method of recording and studying human movement which has been used by work study investigators for many years. It is only in recent years, however, that this technique has been applied to the study of human movement in such sports as golf, athletics and more recently for the recording and analysis of gymnastic moves.

The method consists essentially of attaching a small electric light bulb or bulbs to the part or parts of the body the analyst is interested in studying. The bulbs are powered by a small battery which is fixed to the waist of the gymnast by a belt. During the move to be studied, the bulb is switched on, and a photographic plate exposed for the duration of the move. The bulb may be made to emit a constant light, or to flash on and off at predetermined time intervals. When the light is continuous, a 'cyclegraphic' trace of the light path will be recorded on the photographic plate as continuous ribbons of light, which trace the movements of the body parts. If an interrupter is included in the electric circuit, the bulb/bulbs can be flashed on and off at a predetermined and preselected frequency. From the picture obtained, the time taken for the move, or parts of the move, can be determined, as well as the velocity and acceleration of the body parts at different instances. The photographic trace obtained in this case is not continuous but broken, and is called a chronocyclegraph. Ready-made compact lightweight units are commercially available, and these can be strapped to the gymnast without restricting movement.

The traces on the photographic plate can be used to study the movement of the body part that the bulb is attached to. If, for example, the bulb is set to flash at f flashes per second, the time taken between successive flashes is $1/f$ seconds. Therefore, if there are n flash intervals during the move (or part of the move) being studied, then the time taken will equal n/f seconds.

Consider the chronocyclegraphic trace shown in Fig. 78. There are 20 flashes of the bulb per second which has been preset, i.e. $f = 20$. There are 10 intervals between flashes, i.e. $n = 10$. Therefore, the time taken to move from A to B = $n/f = 10/20 = \frac{1}{2}$ second. It is important to note that the flashes appear in a pear-shaped (or tadpole-shaped) form as shown, and the direction of movement will be from the head to the tail of the tadpole.

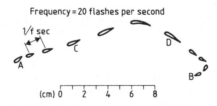

Figure 78 Chronocyclegraphic trace

The body part velocity at any instance during the move can be determined by multiplying the distance between successive flashes, by the frequency of flash f. The velocity between C and D, which is reasonably constant (as the distance between the flashes is constant), would be $\dfrac{8 \times 20}{3}$ (as there are three flash intervals and the distance travelled is approximately 8 cm), i.e. 53 cm/s or 0.53 m/s.

The acceleration or deceleration of body parts can also be

identified and calculated from the chronocyclegraphic trace. If the distance between successive flashes is increasing, then the velocity is increasing and the body part is accelerating. Conversely, if the distance between successive flashes is decreasing, the body part is decelerating.

The main advantage this method of study has over conventional cinematographic methods, lies in the fact that the glider paths are produced on one film, and the laborious task of superimposing successive frames to obtain the glider paths is eliminated.

Chronocyclegraphic traces of five different parts of the body of a gymnast (ankle, knee, hip, shoulder and head) performing a double back somersault tucked dismount from the parallel bars are shown in Fig. 79 (page 122). As well as the glider paths of the body parts, accelerations and decelerations can also be identified. Obviously if a second camera was used to film the move end on (i.e. along the length of the bars) a full three-dimensional effect could be obtained. The position of the gymnast at two instants during the move has been photographed by illuminating the gymnast at these points with a photographic flash.

The use of this photographic method has obvious limitations. Subdued lighting is required to enable the chronocyclegraphic traces to be obtained and so this method is not suitable for recording moves when a dark environment would be dangerous for the execution of the movement. Also this technique would not be suitable for recording an acrobatic series of moves on the floor, as the gymnast would pass out of the photographic range of the stationary camera.

Stroboscopic Studies

People are frequently puzzled as to why the wheels of a movie stagecoach appear to stand still while the coach is moving, or even appear to revolve in the wrong direction. This effect is an optical illusion called stroboscopy which comes from the Greek *strobos* (whirling) and *skopos* (view). The explanation is that the successive frames of the camera stop, or freeze, the spokes of the wheel at the instant the frame is exposed.

The phenomenon can also be produced when a moving object is viewed while being illuminated by an interrupted or flashing light. The principle is similar to the chronocyclegraphic method in that a flashing light source, dark environment and photographic plate are required, but differs in that the gymnast is illuminated by a flashing light at predetermined time intervals during the movement being recorded. The light source used is called a stroboscope or strobo-flood (for very high intensity illumination), and the time interval

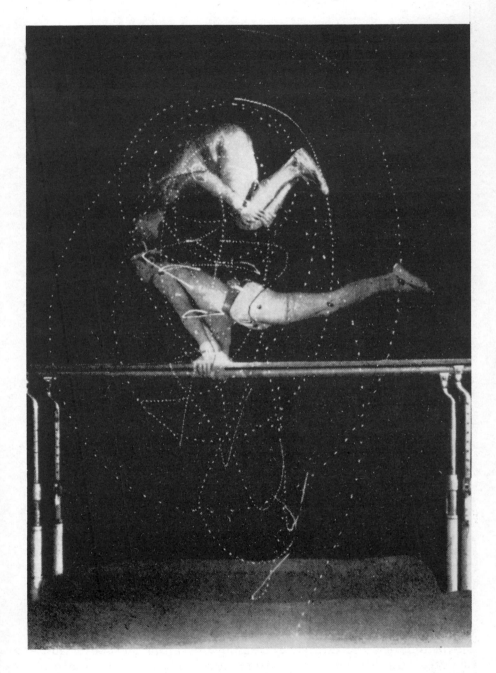

Figure 79 Chronocyclegraphic trace of a gymnast performing a double back somersault tuck dismount from the parallel bars

between flashes can be varied over a wide range (usually from less than one to over a hundred flashes per second). Fig. 80 shows a gymnast photographed by this method while performing a giant swing forward on the high bar. There have been ten flashes of the stroboscope during the three-quarters of the circle photographed. The camera shutter has been opened when the gymnast is just past the vertical handstand position and closed when the gymnast reached the horizontal or 3 o'clock position. Obviously the shutter must be closed before the gymnast returns to the start position or photographs of the second circle will be superimposed over those of

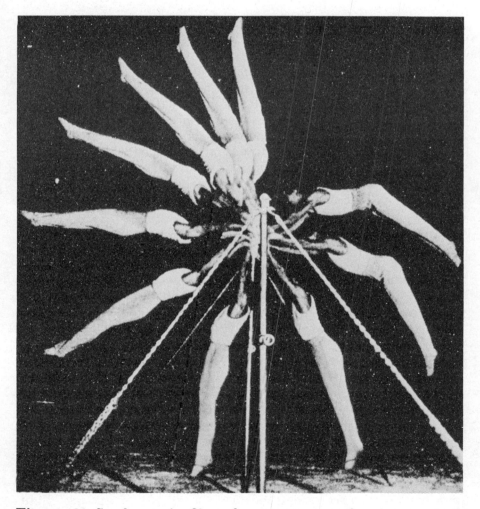

Figure 80 Stroboscopic film of a gymnast performing a giant swing forward on the high bar

the first. A complete record of the move on one photograph is invaluable to coach and performer for a detailed study of the execution of the move. Again the working area has to be darkened as much as possible while still allowing the gymnast sufficient light for safe working. The full potential of this photographic method has not yet been exploited. In addition to providing a powerful diagnostic aid for coach and performer, stroboscopic photographs enable the researcher to determine velocity and acceleration of different body parts during the execution of a move, and hence estimate the magnitude and direction of the forces and turning moments being generated.

Selcom System 700

The use of cinematographic methods for studying gymnastic moves is very laborious and time-consuming. A frame-by-frame study and analysis of the skill is required, and if a high speed camera is being used to obtain good quality photographs (say 200 frames per second) for studying giant swings when the maximum terminal velocity of the body approaches 13 m/s, the analysis can be very protracted.

Fortunately, systems have now been developed which eliminate the necessity for manual calculations and analyses. A system which seems to offer exciting prospects for the future of gymnastics research is the Selcom System 700. Very small infra-red light emitters can be attached to the various parts of the gymnast's body and using two infra-red detecting cameras, a stereo or three-dimensional effect can be produced. The system is capable of monitoring the movements of up to 30 different parts of the body simultaneously (i.e. 30 emitters fixed to the gymnast), and a scan frequency of up to 300 frames per second. The information from the cameras is fed into a computer which is programmed to calculate the relevant body movements in the three axes of movement. These can include velocity, acceleration, position in space, inertia forces, and so on. A practical study situation could be similar to that shown in Fig. 81, designed to study the take-off phase of a vault. For the full three-dimensional capabilities of the system to be exploited, a vault with a twist in the first flight would be the subject of investigation because this involves rotation as well as horizontal and vertical movement.

A force platform or dynamometer capable of measuring horizontal and vertical force components and turning moments due to the initiation of twist at take-off is attached to the reuther board. The two cameras are arranged in such a way that take-off and first flight (i.e. the phase of the vault of interest to the study) are within the measuring range of both cameras. Diodes are attached to the

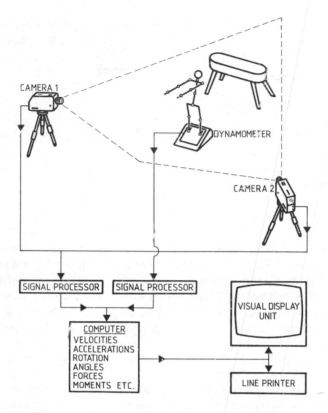

Figure 81 A practical study situation

gymnast's body, preferably at relevant joint positions (knee, hip, and so on, as the movement of any part of the thigh can be determined from readings at these two points). The output signals from both cameras and load platform are fed into a process signaller which transforms the information into a form suitable for processing by the computer. The output results from the computer can take two forms, printed results for permanent record on a line printer (fast typewriter), or results displayed visually on a visual display unit (T.V. screen).

The potential of such a study situation is enormous. With a force dynamometer attached to the top of the horse to investigate thrust forces (and turning moments where relevant), and another force platform to analyse landing, vaults could be analysed in their totality. Obviously similar study situations could be designed to analyse floor agilities and moves on all gymnastic apparatus.

The study of and coaching approach to the sport of gymnastics is becoming more scientific daily and the recent trends in this direction are likely to accelerate in the future.

Theoretical Analysis

Dismounts from the High Bar in Men's Gymnastics

As dismounts from the high bar in men's gymnastics continue to increase in complexity, the safety margin available to the gymnast decreases. Hence an analysis of these moves is not only interesting from a mechanical viewpoint but also essential to identify the variables that contribute to, and the conditions necessary for, their successful and safe execution. This section presents some of the results obtained from a computer-based theoretical study of high bar dismounts. The application of these results and usefulness to coaches is discussed. Finally, the effects of variations in techniques used during the execution of these moves is considered together with the effects they are likely to have on the theoretical predictions.

DEFINITION OF THE PROBLEM

When dismounting from the high bar, the gymnast wishes release to occur at the moment which will allow him to reach the maximum height possible (consistent with the skill being performed) which will give maximum time in the air to perform twists and/or somersaults. However, everything else being equal, the more height the gymnast achieves during the dismount the nearer will be the flight path of his centre of gravity (G) to the bar during descent, thus increasing the risk of hitting the bar. Hence the problem facing the coach and gymnast is one of determining a balance between two of the factors which contribute to the element of risk in the dismount. Extra time in the air, which contributes to a safe execution, can only be achieved at the expense of having flight path distance approaching nearer to the bar. The moment at which the gymnast releases from the bar is one of the critical considerations, together with speed of angular rotation at release. The execution of the dismount will also be affected by individual technique, e.g. changes in body shape prior to release, and energy transfer from bar to gymnast and vice versa.

To provide a theoretical basis of understanding of the factors involved, several simplifying assumptions are made. This helps to facilitate a general analysis.

These assumptions are as follows:

1 The effects of energy losses due to air resistance on the gymnast's body, and sliding friction between the gymnast's hands and bar have been ignored.

2 At release the gymnast applies no force to the bar (i.e. the gymnast simply lets go).

3 Energy transfer from the bar to the gymnast through bar deformation (strain energy) is ignored.

4 The gymnast's body shape is assumed to stay straight prior to and at release from the bar (i.e. the centre of gravity of the gymnast is moving in a circular path of constant radius from the bar).

The effects of these assumptions on the theoretical predictions will be discussed later.

If we divide a circle drawn around the high bar into four quadrants as shown in Fig. 82 (a), it can be seen that dismounts can be classified into two groups, depending on when release occurs. For a gymnast rotating in a counter-clockwise direction release can occur either in quadrant 1 (3 o'clock to 6 o'clock) as in Fig. 82 (b)

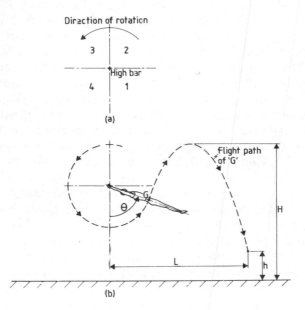

Figure 82 (a) and (b) High bar release angles for dismounts

when the dismount is carried away from the bar, or in quadrant 2 (12 o'clock to 3 o'clock), as in Fig. 82 (c) when the dismount passes back over the bar. The direction in which G moves at the moment of release will be tangential (at right angles) to the arc describing the

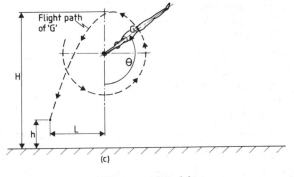

Figure 82 (c)

movement of G at release. For both cases it should be noted that once release has occurred the only external influence acting on the gymnast is gravity and so the flight path of the centre of gravity is completely determined and cannot be influenced by the gymnast. This flight path will be parabolic in nature, and as it can be described in precise mathematical terms it can be analysed. Although the gymnast can twist and/or somersault about this flight path he can do nothing to alter its shape. (This is of course true of the path of the centre of gravity of a gymnast for all flight moves in gymnastics, first and second flight of vault, bar and beam dismounts, and all aerial moves on the floor can be analysed in the same way.) Hence the vertical height (H) achieved by the gymnast (centre of gravity), horizontal distance of landing away from the bar (L), and the time the gymnast will be in the air (T) are (for a given body position at landing) completely determined by the conditions at release (see Fig. 82).

The effects of the timing of release on the trajectory of the flight path of the centre of gravity are shown in Fig. 83. In both cases, it can be seen that height and time are gained at the expense of distance from the bar. Although both groups of dismounts have been studied by the author, this discussion concentrates on quadrant 1 release dismounts as they predominate.

QUADRANT 1 DISMOUNTS
For this group of dismounts, greater height is achieved through a later release, and as the time the gymnast is in the air is dependent only on the height achieved (for a given body position on landing) a late release is obviously desirable for advanced skills. However, the flight path of the centre of gravity approaches nearer to the bar if release occurs later. Conversely an early release carries the gymnast safely away from the bar, but at the expense of height and

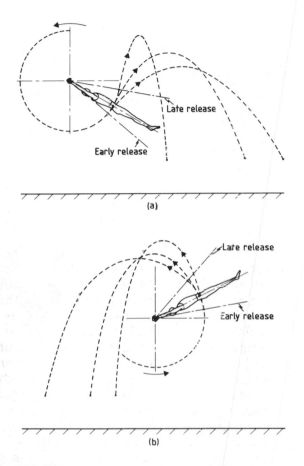

Figure 83 The effect of release angle on dismount trajectory path

therefore less time is available to the gymnast to complete the skill being performed. The importance of buying time will be appreciated when one realises that a difference of half a rotation (perfect landing or complete disaster) in a triple back somersault dismount can be as little as a quarter of a second. Some of the dismounts now being performed are shown in Fig. 84. From what was said earlier, it should be noted that the analysis (in terms of dismount height, length and time in the air) is identical for all these dismounts.

The path of the centre of gravity of the gymnast (and hence height, length and time) will be greatly influenced not only by the angle at which release occurs, but also by the angular velocity (speed of rotation) of the gymnast at release. This in turn, for any

(a) Straight back somersault dismount

(b) Full in back out somersault dismount

(c) Full twisting double back somersault dismount

(d) Triple back somersault dismount

Figure 84 High bar dismounts

given release angle will depend on the angular velocity of the gymnast as he passes vertically over the bar, i.e. the rotational speed through which the gymnast passes the vertical (12 o'clock) position in the giant circle immediately preceding the dismount. This process of increasing the angular velocity or 'winding up' the giant circles leading up to the dismount is an essential feature of modern high bar work. To investigate this effect, the angular velocity of the gymnast (ω, *omega*) passing through the vertical (12 o'clock) position in the circle immediately prior to release has been analysed for a range of angular velocities from a stationary handstand position $\omega = 0$ radian per second (rad/s) up to $\omega = 3$ rad/s, the sort of wind-up velocity required for a triple back somersault dismount. (*Note*: 1 revolution per second is equal to 2π or approximately 6 rad/s)

Angles of release θ measured from the 6 o'clock position, as shown in Fig. 82 (b), from 60° to 90° in 5° intervals, have been investigated for angular velocities ω of 0, 1, 2 and 3 rad/s. The effects on dismount height, length and time are presented in Tables 4–7 (pages 134–6). These results were calculated by a computer programmed to solve the relevant mathematical equations derived by the author (see Appendix 3, page 161). The computer also produced a plot of the associated trajectory paths of the centre of gravity of the gymnast and these are shown in Figs 85 to 88. The computer was also programmed to produce trajectory flight paths for the release

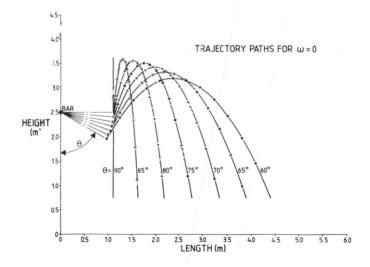

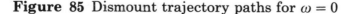

Figure 85 Dismount trajectory paths for $\omega = 0$

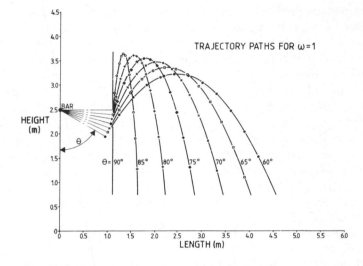
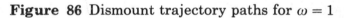

Figure 86 Dismount trajectory paths for $\omega = 1$

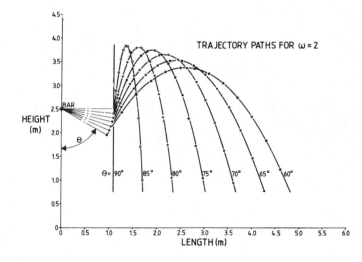
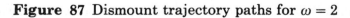

Figure 87 Dismount trajectory paths for $\omega = 2$

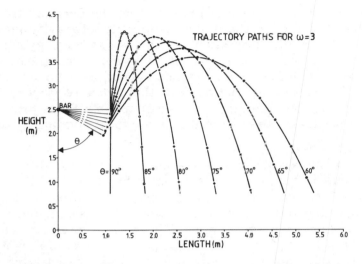

Figure 88 Dismount trajectory paths for $\omega = 3$

angles analysed under different conditions of 'wind up'. A sample output for release angle $\theta = 80°$ is shown in Fig. 89 for $\omega = 0, 1, 2$ and 3 rad/s (see also Table 8). From the diagram on which the analysis is based (Fig. 101 in Appendix 3), it will be noted that the results obtained will be influenced by both the morphology of the gymnast

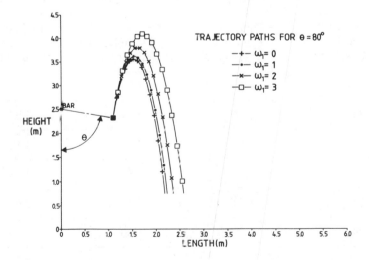

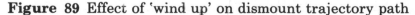

Figure 89 Effect of 'wind up' on dismount trajectory path

(i.e. the distance of centre of gravity from the bar) and the body position on landing (i.e. the height of the centre of gravity above the ground). The results presented are for an 'average gymnast' of height 1·67 m whose distance of centre of gravity from the bar (*X*) is 1·1 m when swinging in an extended position, who achieves a technically acceptable landing with the centre of gravity 0·75 m above the floor on landing (*Y*). It is a simple matter to alter these values to produce a personalised analysis for individual gymnasts.

DISCUSSION OF RESULTS

A study of the results produces some interesting findings. If the dismount starts from a vertical stationary handstand position $\omega = 0$ (closely associated with young gymnasts in the early stages of performing dismounts from giant circles), then maximum time in the air would occur when release is in the horizontal position $\theta = 90°$ ($T = 1.22$ s), but as the flight path of the c. of g. would go vertically up and down and dangerously close to the bar, this would not be a practical release point. The difference between a release angle θ of 70° and 60° gains the gymnast 0.05 seconds in the air and the dismount is still carried safely away from the bar (see Fig. 85, flight path trajectories). The difference between a release of 80° and 70°, however, only gains a further 0.01 second and this gain is clearly no compensation for the danger or having the flight path so much closer to the bar (again see Fig. 85) that a marginal error of release of timing could result in a young inexperienced gymnast coming back on to the bar.

TABLE 4
Angular velocity $\omega = 0$ rad/s

Angle of release θ (degrees)	Time in the air T (seconds)	Length of dismount L (metres)	Maximum height H (metres)
60	1.15	4.24	3.18
65	1.18	3.77	3.32
70	1.20	3.25	3.42
75	1.21	2.70	3.50
80	1.21	2.14	3.57
85	1.22	1.60	3.59
90	1.22	1.10	3.61

TABLE 5
Angular velocity $\omega = 1$ rad/s

Angle of release θ (degrees)	Time in the air T (seconds)	Length of dismount L (metres)	Maximum height H (metres)
60	1.16	4.35	3.23
65	1.20	3.87	3.37
70	1.22	3.32	3.48
75	1.23	2.76	3.56
80	1.24	2.18	3.61
85	1.24	1.62	3.65
90	1.25	1.10	3.67

TABLE 6
Angular velocity $\omega = 2$ rad/s

Angle of release θ (degrees)	Time in the air T (seconds)	Length of dismount L (metres)	Maximum height H (metres)
60	1.20	4.68	3.37
65	1.24	4.16	3.52
70	1.27	3.57	3.65
75	1.29	2.95	3.73
80	1.30	2.31	3.80
85	1.30	1.69	3.83
90	1.31	1.10	3.85

TABLE 7
Angular velocity $\omega = 3$ rad/s

Angle of release θ (degrees)	Time in the air T (seconds)	Length of dismount L (metres)	Maximum height H (metres)
60	1.28	5.22	3.60
65	1.32	4.64	3.77
70	1.35	3.98	3.91
75	1.37	3.25	4.02
80	1.38	2.53	4.09
85	1.39	1.80	4.14
90	1.39	1.10	4.16

The results presented in Tables 5–7 and Fig. 86–88 for $\omega = 1, 2$ and 3 rad/s represent conditions when the circles preceding dismount are used to 'wind up' or increase the angular velocity of the gymnast at release and hence obtain more time to facilitate more complex skills. Later release provides more time in the air but again at the expense of the trajectory path of the dismount approaching closer to the bar. The difference between a release of 70° and 60° for $\omega = 1$ rad/s is 0.06 seconds in the air ($T = 1.22$ and 1.16 seconds respectively), whereas for releases of 80° and 70° the difference is 0.02 second, a larger compensation by 0.01 seconds than for $\omega = 0$ rad/s, but the trajectory path is not carried a great deal further away from the bar (i.e. L = 2.14 m and 2.18 m for $\omega = 0$ and $\omega = 1$ rad/s and $\theta = 80°$).

The results for $\omega = 2$ rad/s and 3 rad/s can be interpreted in the same way. Increased 'wind up' speed gives more time in the air for the gymnast for the same release angle and also carries the dismount further away from the bar. The difference between a release of 70° and 60° gains the gymnast 0.07 seconds and the difference between 80° and 70° an extra 0.03 seconds for $\omega = 3$ rad/s. However, for a release of 80° the horizontal distance of landing away from the bar has increased to 2.53 metres. The extra gain of only 3/100ths of a second at first sight might not seem adequate compensation for a 10° later release which increases the danger of coming back on to the bar if release is mistimed (see Fig. 88). However, the following will demonstrate that at the top level of performance we are, in fact, talking about hundredths of a second. If a triple back somersault dismount is performed from a release angle of say 80° for $\omega = 3$ rad/s, then the gymnast has 1.38 seconds in the air to complete what is effectively $2\frac{3}{4}$ rotations about the transverse axis. Ignoring the time required to close and open body angles immediately prior to release and before landing, this represents less than 0.5 seconds per somersault. Therefore 100th of a second can make a difference of over 7° of body rotation. The .03 second gained from a release of $\theta = 80°$ instead of $\theta = 70°$ corresponds to approximately 22° of rotation and could clearly represent the difference between a good landing and a fall.

A comparison of the effects of increasing 'wind up' for a given release angle of $\theta = 80°$ is given in Table 8 and the associated trajectory paths are shown in Fig. 89. Increasing 'wind up' speed has a dramatic effect on time in the air from 1.21 to 1.39 seconds respectively for $\omega = 0$ to $\omega = 3$ rad/s. Dismount height increases from 3.56 to 4.09 metres and dismount length increases from 2.14 to 2.53 metres. Time in the air increases and the distance the gymnast

TABLE 8
Effect of 'wind up' on dismount flight path parameters for release angle $\theta = 80°$

	Wind up ω (rad/s)			
	0	1	2	3
Time T (seconds)	1.21	1.24	1.30	1.38
Hight H (metres)	3.56	3.61	3.80	4.09
Length L (metres)	2.14	2.18	2.31	2.53

is carried away from the bar increases. Again, the increases in time achieved through 'wind up' should be related to the argument just proposed of time against rotation. A cautionary note should, however, be included. There is a negative factor. As speed of 'wind up' increases, the time available to the gymnast for margin of error at release decreases. The effect of this is shown in Table 9. The figures in the table have been determined by computer analysis and can be interpreted in the following way. The times quoted are the times it will take the gymnast to reach the horizontal position, ($\theta = 90°$) from a given angle (θ) and for a given 'wind up' speed. For example, for $\omega = 3$ and a planned release angle of $\theta = 85°$, if the gymnast releases .017 seconds too late, release will occur at $\theta = 90°$, that is in the horizontal (disaster) position. This means the gymnast

TABLE 9

Effect of 'wind up' on time margin for release

Angle of release	Margin of error in time of release (seconds)			
θ	$\omega = 0$	1	2	3
60	.113	.111	.102	.096
65	.096	.094	.086	.081
70	.078	.077	.070	.066
75	.060	.059	.053	.051
80	.041	.040	.036	.035
85	.022	.021	.018	.017
90	0	0	0	0

has a margin of error of less than 2/100ths of a second. (Note that we are again talking in hundredths of a second.) However, if release was planned for 80° then release would have to be mistimed (delayed) by .035 seconds before actual release would occur in the horizontal (3 o'clock) position. The rest of the figures in the table can be interpreted in the same way, and demonstrate clearly that as speed of 'wind up' increases and release angle increases, the margin of error at release decreases.

It is also interesting to note the effect 'wind up' has on the maximum centrifugal force to which the gymnast is subjected. For $\omega = 0$, i.e. a circle starting from the stationary handstand position, maximum centrifugal force approximately equals four times body weight $(4W)$ and occurs at the bottom of the swing (6 o'clock), when the angular velocity is maximum. Increasing ω has the following effect on maximum centrifugal force.

ω	Maximum centrifugal force
0	$4.0\,W$
1	$4.1\,W$
2	$4.4\,W$
3	$5.1\,W$

RELATION TO PRACTICAL DISMOUNT TECHNIQUES

As the technique adopted even by top gymnasts performing the same dismount shows variations (sometimes only subtle differences, but occasionally marked differences), it is impossible to incorporate these into a general study of this nature which is concerned with producing a basic understanding of the effects of changes in major variables. However, to provide stimulation for coaches and performers and in the hope of promoting discussion, three specific examples of dismounts will be examined and these relate to the figurine drawings shown in Fig. 84 (page 140).

Fig. 84(a) shows a straight back somersault dismount. In the vertical (12 o'clock) position, a straight body position achieves maximum potential energy with the centre of gravity the maximum distance away from the bar. The slight dish shape in the middle of quadrant 3 (to facilitate the leg acceleration later) brings the centre of gravity in towards the bar. In the horizontal (9 o'clock) position, the body shape is again straight (maximising the turning moment due to gravity). During quadrant 4, the hips lead giving a hollow body position again bringing G closer to the bar. By the vertical hang (6 o'clock) position, the legs have accelerated and caught up with the upper body, producing a near straight body position. The legs continue to lead the upper body into quadrant 1 and again G moves nearer to the high bar. The effect of these body changes on the path of movement of the centre of gravity are shown in Fig. 90(a) and will obviously affect the theoretical results predicted which assumed G to move in a path of a constant radius. However, for performers of high quality, the changes in body angles are small and the theoretical results obtained will give a close approximation to the execution of this dismount.

Fig. 84(b) shows a straight back somersault dismount with full twist followed by a tuck back somersault (i.e. a full in back out), and again, for the reasons quoted above, the results obtained from the theoretical analysis should show a close approximation to the practical execution of this advanced dismount. Again the path of G will be similar to that shown in Fig. 90(a). The same reasoning can be applied to straight back somersault dismounts with multiple twists and straight front somersault dismounts.

Fig. 84(c) shows a full twisting double back somersault and here there is a pronounced change in body shape during quadrant 1. The gymnast anticipates the dismount and starts to shorten the body length (moment of inertia), preparing for the somersault before release occurs. This has two effects: it changes the path of movement of the centre of gravity and produces an increase in the angular velocity compared with that which would be achieved if the gymnast maintained a straight body position. This is shown in a

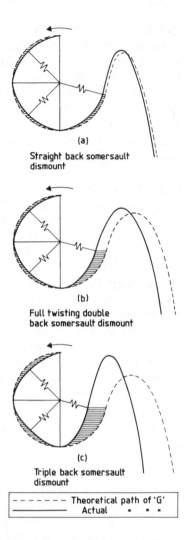

(a)

Straight back somersault
dismount

(b)

Full twisting double
back somersault dismount

(c)

Triple back somersault
dismount

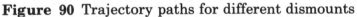

– – – – – – – Theoretical path of 'G'
――――― Actual   ▪ ▪ ▪

Figure 90 Trajectory paths for different dismounts

simplified form in Fig. 90(b), where it can be seen that shortening
alters the direction of the centre of gravity at release and hence the
flight path trajectory. Release can occur earlier than if a straight
body is maintained, without losing height and hence time.

A study of photographic evidence of triple back somersault
dismounts shows a pronounced shortening of the body prior to
release (for example, see Fig. 84(d)), far more pronounced than for

the full twisting double back somersault just discussed. This is to be expected as the gymnast is only concerned with rotation about the transverse axis, whereas in the previous dismount which involved rotation about the two axes (transverse and longitudinal) a reduction in the moment of inertia about the transverse (somersault) axis increases the moment of inertia about the longitudinal axis and inhibits twisting. The effect of this shortening can be seen in Fig. 90(c). Hence for a given release angle, the trajectory path of G is much shorter and higher than for release at the same angle with a straight body.

Energy losses due to air resistance on the gymnast's body and sliding friction between the gymnast's hands and bar will also affect the theoretical predictions, but their effects are small (estimated at less than 5%). Although they will marginally reduce the predicted values for length, height and time, the ratio of these values will stay approximately the same and should therefore not affect the overall conclusions derived. The effects are largely cancelled out by the energy inputs from the gymnast (i.e. through changing of body angles).

It should be emphasised that the information provided here does not represent the complete picture, but is intended to provide a platform of knowledge on which the coach can build. Because of the assumptions made in the theoretical analysis, the results obtained should be interpreted carefully. The effects of individual techniques used for different dismounts has been discussed, and it is hoped that this will stimulate the reader to reconsider in a new light the effects of the techniques advocated in terms of body shape prior to release, release angle, wind-up speed and time achieved for the dismount.

It has been clearly demonstrated that for advanced dismounts the margin of safety available to the gymnast on the timing of release is extremely small, only hundredths of a second separating a fall on landing (too early a release) from the gymnast coming back on to the bar (too late a release). The analysis suggests that release angles of greater than 80° should not be recommended, as the maximum time gain available for the dismount is only one hundredth of a second, and this is not a sufficient recompense for having a margin of error at release reduced to under three hundredths of a second.

These are results that coaches should consider carefully in designing training programmes to progress gymnasts to the advanced skills. Repeatability both of circles prior to release and of release conditions to within very fine time limits are essential for the safe execution of advanced dismounts.

8

The Vault

In the preceding chapters, various aspects of the vault have been considered. The object of this chapter is to bring together all the parts of the vault previously discussed and to study the move as a whole. The reason why vaulting has been singled out for special treatment, is that it represents the total exercise on the vaulting horse and ten marks can be scored for the execution of one move.

Three vaults have been chosen for detailed study, and all three vaults are applicable to both men's and women's gymnastics.

1   The *hecht vault* as an example of the class of vaults when rotation in the second flight is in an opposite direction to first flight rotation. Other examples of counter-rotation vaults include straddle, stoop and through vaults.

2   The *Yamashita* as an example of the class of vaults that require a 360° rotation of the body about the transverse axis, i.e. second flight rotation is in the same direction as first flight. Other examples include handspring and cartwheel vaults.

3   The *Tsukahara* as an example of a vault that requires body rotation about two axes: a twist and a somersault.

The Hecht Vault

The complete vault is shown in Fig. 91. At the commencement of the run-up the gymnast has no energy. As the speed of run-up increases the kinetic energy of the gymnast increases and should reach the maximum value about 2 or 3 strides from the reuther board. The gymnast will then possess kinetic energy of $\frac{1}{2}mv^2$, where v is the velocity of approach of the gymnast at the reuther board. On impact with the board the gymnast has a forward momentum of M_2 and does work in deforming or compressing the board. Hence some of the kinetic energy is converted into strain energy. This must be accompanied by a reduction in the horizontal velocity of the

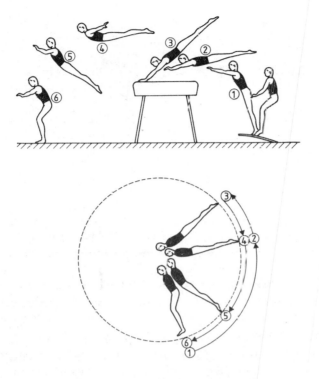

Figure 91 The hecht vault

gymnast (the total energy must remain the same). During take-off, the strain energy stored in the board is returned (or at least nearly all of it is; there will be frictional losses) to the gymnast in such a way as to alter the direction and velocity of the gymnast. This is also supplemented by a strong thrust from the gymnast's legs, F. There is an associated thrust momentum M_1 acting through G parallel to F. The direction and speed of movement of the centre of gravity of the gymnast at take-off will be governed by the resultant M_R of M_1 and M_2, and the speed of body rotation will be governed by the magnitude of the turning moment, $F \times r$ (Fig. 92), i.e. the larger the turning moment, the faster will be the rotation. Note that the arm action assists elevation during take off. The arms are swung vigorously forwards and upwards during take off. It should be noted that although currently there is much discussion and theorising on board take-off techniques, length and height of hurdle step, fast or slow pick up of the trailing leg, and so on, there is no practical evidence to demonstrate that optimum take-off conditions have

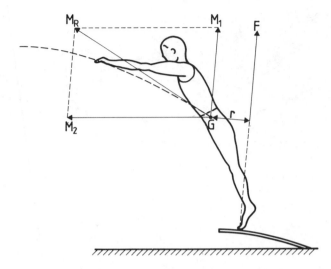

Figure 92 Analysis of vault take-off

been established. This represents an important field for investigation. After all, in terms of scoring, vault take-off is probably the most important 0.1 to 0.15 seconds in gymnastics.

The path of the centre of gravity during the first flight will be parabolic and the body will rotate in an anticlockwise direction about the centre of gravity as shown, until the hands contact the horse, i.e. from position 1 to position 3 (Fig. 91). During the first flight phase, some of the kinetic energy of the body is changed into potential energy as the gymnast rises above the horse. Hence the vertical (upward) velocity component is reducing under the action of gravity. The horizontal velocity component will (if we neglect air resistance) remain the same during first flight. These individual aspects of the vault have all been dealt with earlier.

The magnitude and direction of the thrust (F) on the horse is all-important (Fig. 93). The thrust must pass in front of the centre of gravity of the gymnast to produce the clockwise turning moment necessary to change the direction of body rotation. This will also have an associated momentum vector M_1. For this to be possible, the hands must be well ahead of the shoulders, and a body position near to horizontal is required. The eccentric thrust has a value of $F \times r$ and is responsible for reversing the direction of body rotation from position 3 to position 6 (Fig. 91). The momentum resultant M_R determines the velocity and direction of the centre of gravity during second flight. Obviously a large turning moment is required to reverse the direction of rotation of the gymnast during the vault.

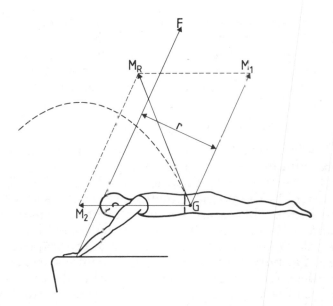

Figure 93 Analysis of the thrust phase of a hecht vault

This can be achieved by increasing either F or r or both. Strong straight arm thrust strength is therefore necessary for this vault, i.e. this is a high thrust vault. The straight arm press exercises using bathroom scales, discussed previously, would be useful here.

The trajectory path of the centre of gravity of the gymnast during second flight will again be parabolic. The velocity and direction of the centre of gravity at departure from the horse will be governed by the resultant momentum vector M_R (i.e. the resultant obtained by vectorially adding M_1 and M_2, using the parallelogram of forces).

During second flight, therefore, the gymnast continues to lose kinetic energy with an increasing gain in potential energy until the highest point of the flight is reached. During descent to the ground, the gymnast loses all of the potential energy which is converted back to kinetic energy in the form of increased velocity. Finally to achieve a good landing, all of the kinetic energy must be absorbed on impact with the ground by using the knees as shock absorbers.

The Yamashita Vault

The emphasis in vault judging in recent years has changed. The main emphasis is now placed on second flight. This is, of course, understandable as we have seen the introduction of vaults with twists, somersaults and a combination of both in second flight. For the gymnast to perform these advanced skills, it is essential that the vaulter is in the air as long as possible during the second flight phase. To achieve this, high flight paths of the centre of gravity of the gymnast are required. This has been discussed earlier. Remember:

HEIGHT = TIME = SAFETY

If we refer back briefly to the discussion on the thrust phase of an overswing vault in Chapter 3 (Figs. 25 and 26), we will see that extra height in the second flight can be achieved by a greater thrust from the gymnast, or by the gymnast having a lower trajectory first flight on to the horse. This is an over-simplification. There are other factors that will affect the direction of the trajectory path of the second flight. These include the direction of the trajectory path of the centre of gravity of the gymnast when contact first occurs with the horse, the effects of action/reaction within the gymnast's body and changes of body angles, and the effect of the centrifugal force acting on the gymnast, produced by the pivotal body rotation during the thrust phase. These factors will now be considered in the analysis of the Yamashita vault.

Although the individual techniques of great vaulters show slight variations, we will emphasise here the points of similarity that are essential for the production of a good Yamashita vault.

What was said about the Hecht vault regarding run-up speed, parabolic paths of the centre of gravity of the body during first and second flight, and energy conversion, apply to all vaults and will not be reiterated here.

The strike angle (i.e. body angle measured above the horizontal) with the horse should occur at a low angle usually varying between 30° and 45°. The angle of strike will depend, among other things, on the thrust strength of the gymnast, the speed of body rotation during first flight (which depends on foot speed off the reuther board), and the direction of the flight path of the centre of gravity when the gymnast makes initial contact with the horse. Stronger gymnasts with fast foot speed from the board can attack the horse at lower strike angles.

Thrust can be considered to consist of two phases: Phase 1, absorption—this will involve shoulder girdle depression; and Phase 2, extension (or repulsion)—this will involve shoulder girdle extension (stretch). One of the gymnast's objectives is to reduce the total contact time with the horse and hence utilise the elastic energy stored in the muscles during absorption to be released during extension, thus utilising what has been described as muscular implant energy. This is similar to utilising energy stored in a spring.

Research suggests that strain energy can only be stored in muscles for less than approximately 0.15 seconds, after which time the stored energy rapidly dissipates. Hence the thrust phase (and all take off activities) should be less than this time.

A diagram showing the body position when the hands first contact the horse is shown in Fig. 94(a). Here a strike angle of approximately 30° is shown. A hollow body position with a hip extension of approximately 200° is shown and an arm extension angle of approximately 150°.

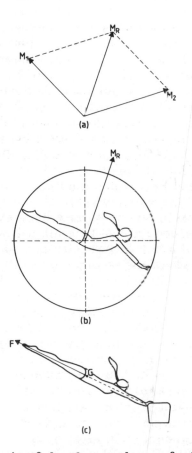

Figure 94 Analysis of the thrust phase of a Yamashita vault

Although there is nothing magic about the angles quoted here, analysis of photographic evidence suggest that some of the best Yamashita vaults are produced from body contact angles similar to those quoted.

During the thrust phase, when the hands are in contact with the horse, the horse acts as the pivot point while the body rotates through approximately 40° to 50°, depending on the strike angle, foot speed, and so on. The direction of the resultant momentum vector M_R at initial impact is obtained by combining the thrust momentum M_1 and the forward body momentum M_2. Note the forward momentum M_2 is not horizontal but inclined upwards, as in Fig. 94(b), the reason being that with a low strike angle the centre of gravity of the gymnast has not reached the top of the parabolic flight curve and is therefore still rising. This will have a vertical component acting upwards which will assist in elevation in the second flight. The hollow body position shown is used to provide a body action/reaction and assists the gymnast in 'snapping' into the deep pike required of the vault. During repulsion, the arm extension increases from approximately 150° to 180° at departure from the horse. This opening of the shoulder angle during the thrust phase forces the centre of gravity of the gymnast further away from the horse and therefore assists in producing a higher second flight of the vault. There is a cautionary note, however, for coaches. Although a hollow body shape in first flight can assist in producing an action/reaction into the pike required in the second flight of the vault, and also assist in producing a higher second flight (for the same reason as opening the shoulder angle, i.e. forcing the centre of gravity further away from the horse during extension), there are associated technical deductions. This analysis will equally apply to handspring one and a half front somersault vaults.

The trajectory path of the second flight will also depend on the gymnast's speed of rotation during the thrust phase. The faster the angular velocity ω, the greater will be the centrifugal force F tending to propel the gymnast away from the horse, as shown in Fig. 94(c). Hence fast body rotation in first flight and therefore during the thrust phase can increase the height of the trajectory path of the second flight.

During second flight, the body will have an angular momentum which will remain constant throughout this free flight phase of the vault. One of the major problems gymnasts encounter during this vault is controlling the body rotation and achieving a good landing. The second flight provides an interesting study in the conservation of angular momentum. From the time the gymnast leaves the horse until landing, there will be a clockwise body rotation and hence clockwise angular momentum. Initially, the rotation occurs in the upper part of the body. The trunk rotates through approximately 90°, while leg rotation has been stopped. Indeed with some gymnasts who have a strong thrust and rapid upper body rotation during this phase, there is a slight counter-rotation of the legs which ensure

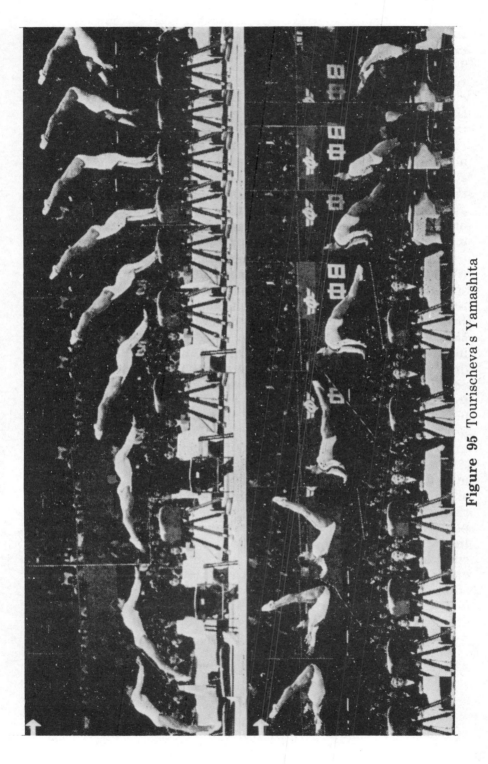

Figure 95 Tourischeva's Yamashita

that too great a clockwise angular rotation is not achieved. This can be seen clearly in the Yamashita vault being performed by Tourischeva in Fig. 95. A study of the vault shows that the very rapid clockwise rotation of the upper body is accompanied by a counter (anticlockwise) rotation of the legs. It can also be noted that, during the thrust phase, there is clear evidence of thrust from the horse and a definite stretch through the shoulders; arm extension has increased from approximately 150° to 180° and is accompanied by a straightening of the slight hollow. After repulsion from the horse, the fold angle is maintained until the trunk is in the horizontal position, i.e. back of the gymnast is parallel to the ground. This is the highest point of the second flight. There is obviously an increase in speed of rotation due to reducing the moment of inertia.

During the descent phase, there must be a rapid clockwise rotation of the legs to open out the fold. While this happens the speed of rotation decreases as the lever length increases. It can be seen that while the legs rotate through approximately 180°, the rotation of the trunk of the body is stopped. In fact, in the vault shown, to counterbalance the very rapid clockwise rotation of the legs the upper part of the body slightly rotates in an anti-clockwise direction. With well-executed Yamashitas like that illustrated, this counter-rotation of the trunk is insufficient on its own to prevent a forward over-rotation during the second flight, and it can be seen clearly that this has to be supplemented by a very vigorous accompanying counter-rotation of the arms to ensure the shoulders are kept back and correct landing body position is achieved.

Finally, let us consider the landing. Contact with the floor will be at point O with the centre of gravity approximately in the position shown in Fig. 96. The path describing the movement of the centre of gravity from position G on initial contact with the floor to the final position G_1 (vertically above O), is shown by the broken line. At the instant of touchdown, the direction of R (floor reaction) will be similar to that shown, i.e. it passes in front of G to produce the anticlockwise turning moment necessary to reduce the clockwise body rotation which will occur as pivotal rotation about the gymnast's feet (contact point with the floor). The rate of pivotal angular deceleration can be estimated from:

$$-mgx = I_0\alpha$$

where I_0 = moment of inertia of gymnast about O.

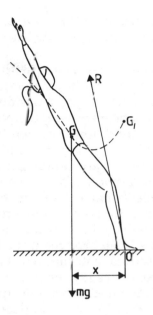

Figure 96 Vault landing position

The Tsukahara Vault

The vault which is currently dominating the women's gymnastic vault scene is named after its originator Mitsuo Tsukahara. The vault consists of a cartwheel or half turn on to the horse in first flight and what is effectively one and a half somersaults in the second flight. There are three variations, the tuck Tsukahara where the somersault is performed with a tuck body position, the piked, and the straight Tsukahara. However, the latter is somewhat of a misnomer because most straight Tsukaharas, even at the top level in women's gymnastics, are usually performed with a hollow body position to reduce the moment of inertia and increase speed of rotation, followed by a pike finish position (i.e. an action/reaction snap of the body).

It was stated earlier that the degree of difficulty of a somersault depends on the body position adopted, the straight Tsukahara being obviously more difficult than the piked because of the higher associated moment of inertia and increased reluctance to rotation. For the same reason the tuck is easier to perform than the piked Tsukahara. To ensure the record is complete, it should be mentioned that full twisting Tsukaharas are now being consistently performed at the top level and pencil straight Tsukaharas have been demonstrated. Some gymnasts and coaches are working on double Tsukaharas.

Variations in technique exist amongst the best vaulters in the performance of a Tsukahara vault which reflect differences in run-up speed, arm and shoulder strength, individual morphology, and so on. Again here we will concentrate on the points of similarity that are essential for a good execution of the vault rather than on slight differences in technique.

The first flight consists of a quarter turn into a cartwheel position (or half turn on) at initial contact with the horse. To achieve this twist, body rotation must be initiated from the reuther board itself, and in addition to having horizontal and vertical force components at take-off (which determines the velocity and trajectory of the first flight) the gymnast must also produce a turning moment from the board to initiate longitudinal rotation. To achieve this, the top half of the body must have already started to rotate against the frictional resistance of the feet while they are still in contact with the board.

The lower the angle of strike, the higher the second flight, provided the gymnast has the necessary strength to produce the required thrust and fast foot speed off the reuther board. We often talk glibly of the thrust phase of a vault as if it is an instantaneous happening. As we saw from the Yamashita vault, during the thrust phase the hands remain in contact with the horse for a period of time, while the body rotates about this fulcrum point. During this phase of the Tsukahara vault, the gymnast produces the additional quarter turn for a cartwheel entry, to complete the 180° longitudinal rotation necessary to be in the correct position to execute the somersault in the second flight. Two angles are important during the thrust phase of the vault: θ_1, the strike angle with the horse, and θ_2, the body angle when the hands leave the horse. Photographic evidence suggests for top female vaulters these angles are in the range:

$$\theta_1 = \text{from } 20° \text{ to } 40°$$

and $$\theta_2 = \text{from } 75° \text{ to } 90°$$

(both angles measured above the horizontal)

What was said about the force analysis of the repulsion stage of the Yamashita vault applies equally here. The parallelogram shown in Fig. 94(a) is again relevant. The low angle of thrust indicates a low strike angle and the upward direction of M_2 indicates that the centre of gravity of the gymnast is still rising at the point of impact with the horse. The combined effect gives a resultant M_R acting upwards near to the vertical position and ensures a high second flight trajectory path. The object of the first flight and thrust phase is to achieve as high a second flight as possible to maximise the time the gymnast is in the air, to enable the somersault (and twist) to be achieved.

A technique used by many top female gymnast to 'block' horizontal momentum and convert it into vertical lift is associated with the placement of the leading hand, which is thrust into the side of the horse as shown in Fig. 97. This effectively checks forward momentum which is converted into second flight elevation. Again a cautionary note: to use this technique the gymnast must have very rapid body rotation during first flight and thrust (to reduce the forces she is subjected to), and have sufficient strength to absorb these forces.

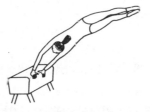

Figure 97 Hand positions during a Tsukahara vault

This type of technique has been demonstrated by some male vaulters, vaulting from the croup of the horse, but an interesting technique to increase second flight elevation is demonstrated in Fig. 98. This is traced from a photograph taken of Tsukahara himself vaulting. Note that the forearm of the leading arm is on the horse itself. During the thrust phase this arm straightens very quickly, forcing the centre of gravity rapidly away from the pivot point (horse). This has the desired effect of producing a higher second flight.

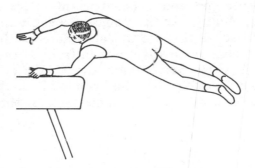

Figure 98 Tsukahara at initial contact with the horse

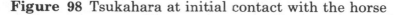

Figure 99 A straight Tsukahara vault

An example of a straight (straight-hollow-pike) Tsukahara is shown in Fig. 99, where the vault was performed by L. Yudina (USSR). Initial contact with the horse occurs at θ_1 about 30° and the gymnast is off the horse just before the vertical, θ_2 approximately 85°. The hollow-pike action is clearly demonstrated, but as the body must pass through a straight position in moving from the hollow to the pike, it does qualify as a straight Tsukahara. This again is a good example of action/reaction (hollow to pike). The objective of the gymnast should be to reduce the variations in body shapes during second flight to a minimum. It should be noted that at initial contact with the horse, the gymnast has only completed a 90° long axis body rotation, and hence it would be described as a cartwheel entry vault.

The body position on landing is important, and the argument put forward about landing from the Yamashita vault applies here, but reversed in the sense that on initial contact with the floor the weight W must pass vertically down in front of the feet, and the ground reaction must pass behind the centre of gravity. This reversal is due to the fact that the gymnast is landing facing the vaulting horse in the Tsukahara and back to the horse in the Yamashita.

9

Implications for Coaching

The diagram Fig. 100 (page 156) is an attempt to lay out, in a formalised and systematic manner, the stages involved in coaching. It is suggested that for coaches faced with a new gymnastic move to be coached for the first time, the approach indicated can provide a useful framework.

The first step in the process is to carry out a mechanical analysis or appraisal of the move to be coached. This will enable the coach to identify the mechanical requirements for the correct and efficient execution of the skill.

This analysis will identify the physical requirements required of the gymnast to execute the move with mechanical and aesthetic correctness and maximum amplitude. The physical requirements of the gymnast can then be stated in terms of strength and range of movements.

If the gymnast does not possess these qualities, then training programmes must be designed to achieve the necessary strength and mobility requirements for success.

In parallel with this process of preparing the gymnast for the skill to be coached, preparation of the coach and relevant training situations should also be developed. The coach should identify the coaching progressions that will be necessary, the spotting techniques that will be used, and give consideration to design of training situations where applicable.

When the gymnast, coach and training situation are all prepared, it is then only a question of progression and repetition.

This system implies a logical and orderly approach to coaching with the long term objectives and expected achievements of the gymnast clearly identified by the coach. Planning to achieve these objectives can then be carried out as suggested.

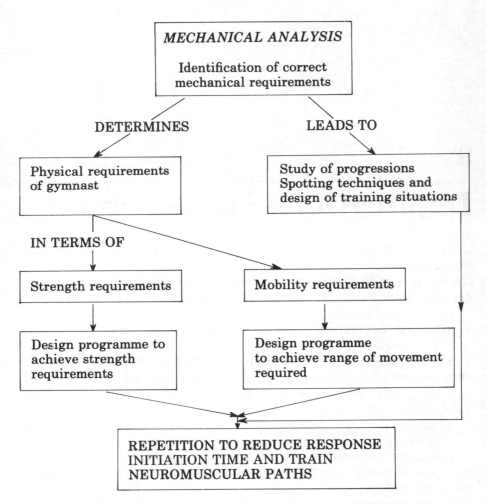

Figure 100 Systematic approach to coaching

Example

By way of a simple example, let us consider coaching a straddle cut and catch on the high bar or the asymmetric bars from rear support position above the high bar. This move has been chosen as it is appropriate to both men's and women's gymnastics.

Objective

Execution of the move with technical exactness and maximum amplitude.

MECHANICAL REQUIREMENT 1
Achieve a position of high potential at the start of the move to store maximum amount of potential energy. It is only in this way that our objective of maximum amplitude can be achieved.

PHYSICAL REQUIREMENT 1
The gymnast achieves an on balance Russian lever position at the commencement of the move. This has obvious implications for range of movement (deep fold) and strength (ability to create the necessary body angles, particularly triceps strength). Design a training programme to achieve these physical requirements.

MECHANICAL REQUIREMENT 2
Maximum conversion of energy during the downswing, i.e. maximum angular velocity of gymnast at bottom of swing. This requires the centre of gravity to be as far away from the bar as possible during and at the bottom of the downswing. Hence the deep fold in the figure 4 position discussed earlier. (Note that this also achieves maximum amplitude.)

Training Implication

Train the gymnast to recognise and feel this position. Progression through backward seat circles, etc.

MECHANICAL REQUIREMENT 3
The gymnast should achieve the highest possible uprise before the straddle cut (again, look for maximum amplitude of the movement).

PHYSICAL REQUIREMENT 2
Straight arm press strength to lift the centre of gravity as high as possible during the uprise. Design a training situation to achieve this (multigym facilities may be useful, or a pulley and weights, bathroom scales, etc.).

MECHANICAL REQUIREMENT 4
The straddle cut and catch should normally be performed in such a way that the gymnast is in a position of as high a potential at the completion of the movement as possible. Again, look for maximum amplitude and the storing of a maximum amount of potential energy to be used to facilitate the execution of the next move (e.g. to short clear circle; World Sets, High Bar, 1972 and 1974).

PHYSICAL REQUIREMENT 3
Appropriate range of movement in the hip joints is essential together with the necessary strength to provide the sufficient leg acceleration required for the cut catch action. Design an appropriate training programme.

Appendix 1

Newton's second law states that the rate of change of momentum is proportional to the applied force and acts along the line of action of the force. Hence, if a force F acts on a particle of mass m which has a velocity v, the rate of change of momentum (mv)

$$= \frac{d}{dt}(mv) = m\left(\frac{dv}{dt}\right) + v\left(\frac{dm}{dt}\right)$$

$$= m\frac{dv}{dt}, \text{ (if } m \text{ is constant)}$$

$$= ma$$

where a is the acceleration. This acceleration is therefore along the line of action of the force F, and we have that F is proportional to ma, that is,

$$F \propto ma$$
$$\therefore F = kma$$

where k is a constant.

Metric System

The metric system now in use is the Systeme International d'Unites (S.I.) in which force is measured in newtons (N) acceleration in metre per second per second (m/s²) and mass in kilogrammes (kg).

A newton is that force which applied to a mass of 1 kg gives it an acceleration of $1\,\text{m/s}^2$.

Appendix 2

When a constant force F acts on a body of mass m for time t and increases its velocity from u to v along the line of action of the force we have:

$$F = ma$$
$$Ft = m(v - u)$$
$$Ft = mv - mu$$
$$= \text{Change in momentum}$$

If the force F is of variable magnitude, we have:

$$F = ma$$

$$F = m\frac{dv}{dt}$$

$$Fdt = m\frac{dv}{dt} dt$$

$$\int_0^t Fdt = \int_0^t m\frac{dv}{dt} dt$$

$$= mv - mu$$
$$= \text{Change of momentum}$$

These formulae measure the change of momentum along the line of action of the force and as was seen in Figure 23 represents the area under the force (thrust) time curve. The formulae are valid for all values of t for which the force is defined and apply to the change of momentum of a rigid body all of whose particles have the same velocity.

The quantity $\int_0^t Fdt$ (or Ft if F is constant) is called the *impulse* acting on the body.

The concept of an impulse is particularly useful when examining thrust phases of gymnastic moves, where by measuring the change of momentum, (say by cinematographic methods), it is possible to estimate the impulse being applied by the gymnast. A cautionary note however. The direction of the force F as well as its magnitude is constantly changing during the thrust phase and the gymnast's body is not a rigid object and hence there will be relative velocities between different body parts. This means that the thrust values determined will only be approximate.

Appendix 3

The analysis used to derive the equations presented below was based on energy considerations, i.e. the total energy possessed by the gymnast at release must equal the energy possessed by the gymnast in the vertical (12 o'clock) position in the circle immediately prior to dismount minus frictional losses plus energy inputs by the gymnast. The following equations have been derived from Fig. 101 on this basis. (*Note*: Frictional losses and energy inputs have been ignored, see assumptions stated earlier.)

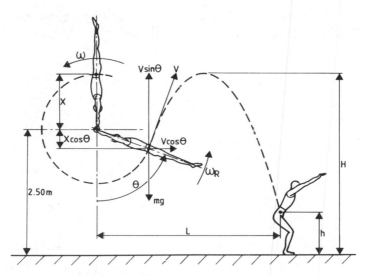

Figure 101 Analysis of high bar dismounts

$$H = Z - X\cos\theta + \frac{v^2}{2g}\sin^2\theta \tag{1}$$

$$T = \frac{v}{g}\sin\theta + \sqrt{\frac{2(H-h)}{g}} \tag{2}$$

$$L = vT\cos\theta + X\sin\theta \tag{3}$$

where H = maximum height of centre of gravity of gymnast above the ground

T = time the gymnast is in the air during dismount
L = horizontal distance of landing from the bar
g = acceleration due to gravity
Z = height of bar (2.50 m)
θ = release angle
X = distance of centre of gravity of gymnast from bar
h = distance of centre of gravity of gymnast above the floor at landing
v = linear velocity of centre of gravity of gymnast at release

i.e. $v = \omega_R X$

where ω_R = angular velocity of gymnast at release

and $\omega_R = \sqrt{\left(\dfrac{2g}{X}(1 + \cos\theta) + \omega^2 \right)}$

where ω = angular velocity of gymnast passing through the vertical (12 o'clock) position in the circle prior to release.

Glossary of Terms Used

ACCELERATION DUE TO GRAVITY
The acceleration of a body falling freely under the action of gravity is constant irrespective of the weight of the body.

ANATOMY
The study of the musculoskeletal system of the human body, the mechanical system responsible for body movement.

ANGULAR ACCELERATION
The rate at which the speed of rotation is increasing or decreasing (deceleration).

ANGULAR MOMENTUM
A quantity of motion possessed by a rotating body which depends on that body's moment of inertia (q.v.) and speed of rotation.

ANGULAR VELOCITY
A measure of the rate at which a body is rotating or spinning.

BIOMECHANICS
The application of the principles of mechanics to the study of human body movement.

CENTRE OF GRAVITY
The point at which, for convenience, all the mass of a body can be considered to act.

CENTRIFUGAL FORCE
A rotating body is subjected to a force tending to throw it away from the point of rotation. This is the centrifugal force which depends on the mass, the speed of rotation and the distance of the centre of gravity of the body from the point of rotation.

CENTRIPETAL FORCE
A restraining reaction to the centrifugal force, supplied by the tension in the gymnast's body resisting release from the apparatus.

CHRONOCYCLEGRAPHIC ANALYSIS
A photographic method of recording gymnastic movements which involves attaching to different parts of the gymnast's body light bulbs which can be programmed to flash on and off at a selected frequency.

DYNAMIC
A situation occurring when the force (or forces) applied to a body are not balanced, and so causes movement of the body to occur.

DYNAMOMETER
A device for measuring the magnitude of an applied force or forces.

ECCENTRIC FORCE
See Turning Moment

ENERGY
The capacity of a body to do work. Energy can be stored in the body in a variety of different ways. *See also* Kinetic Energy; Potential Energy.

FORCE
A push or a pull which when applied to a body will cause or try to cause body movement to occur.

FULCRUM
see Lever

GRAVITY
The attraction or force the earth exerts on all other bodies.

IMPULSE
A product of force and time.

INERTIA
The intrinsic tendency of a body to resist any force trying to move it. *See also* Moment of Inertia.

KINESIOLOGY
The scientific study of human movement which embraces aspects of biomechanics, anatomy and physiology.

KINETIC ENERGY
The energy stored in a body on account of its velocity. The faster a body moves the more kinetic energy it possesses.

LEVER
A solid bar which is pivoted at a fixed point (known as the fulcrum) in such a way that the bar will rotate about the fulcrum if a force is applied to it at a specified point.

LINEAR ACCELERATION
The rate at which the linear velocity is increasing or decreasing (deceleration), i.e. the rate at which a body is speeding up or slowing down.

LINEAR VELOCITY
The rate at which distance is travelled in a straight line, a measure of how fast a body is moving in a specific direction.

MASS
The amount of material or matter which a body possesses.

MECHANICS
A study of the fundamental principles which govern, predict and explain the way in which a body will react to an applied force or forces.

MOMENT OF INERTIA
A measure of the resistance of a body to rotation which depends on its mass and radius of gyration. It relates to the term 'lever' frequently used in gymnastics.

MOMENTUM
A quantity of motion possessed by a moving body and obtained by multiplying the mass of the body by its velocity.

MUSCULOSKELETAL SYSTEM
The arrangement of bones and muscles within the human body.

NEUROMUSCULAR SYSTEM
The system responsible for initiating, monitoring and controlling body movement.

PHYSIOLOGY
The study of the function of the human body: this includes the study of the neuromuscular system of the body, the system responsible for initiating, monitoring and controlling body movement.

POTENTIAL ENERGY
The energy stored in a body on account of its position or height. The higher a body is raised the more potential energy it possesses.

RADIUS OF GYRATION
A measure of how far away from the point of rotation the mass of a rotating body can be considered to act. This again relates to the term 'lever' (q.v.).

RESPONSE INITIATION TIME
A measure of the speed at which a gymnast will respond to a stimulus.

RESULTANT FORCE
If a body is being acted on by several forces simultaneously and they do not cancel one another out, then the resultant force is that one single force which would produce the same effect on the body as the combined effect of all the forces acting together.

STATIC
A situation occurring when all the forces acting on a body cancel one another out. This means the body is in a state of balance.

STRAIN OR ELASTIC ENERGY
The energy stored in a body on account of its deformation under the action of a force, e.g. the more we depress a reuther board, the more strain energy we store in it.

STRENGTH
The ability of the body or part of the body to produce a force.

STROBOSCOPIC ANALYSIS
A photographic method of recording gymnastic movements which requires a high intensity light source that can be flashed on and off at predetermined time intervals periodically illuminating the gymnast during the execution of the move.

TURNING MOMENT OR ECCENTRIC FORCE
A force (q.v.) whose direction does not pass through the centre of gravity of a body. Hence it causes body rotation to occur.

VECTOR
A quantity that has magnitude and direction and can be represented graphically by a straight line.

WEIGHT
The property a body has by reason of it being attracted towards the earth by the force of gravity.
Note: In common use, we confuse weight and mass. Admittedly the weight of a body will depend on its mass, but it is possible for a body to have no weight (e.g. astronauts experience weight loss in space) yet still retain mass. Throughout the book the terms weight and mass are used. Whenever they occur the reader can regard both as having the same meaning without any major distortion of the principles being presented.

Bibliography

BATTERMAN, C. (1968) *The Techniques of Springboard Diving*. Cambridge, Mass.: MIT Press.

BASFORD, L. (1966) *The Science of Movement*. London: Sampson Low.

BEOER, M. R. (1973) *Efficiency of Human Movement*. Philadelphia, Pa.: W. B. Saunders.

BUNN, J. W. (1972) *Scientific Principles of Coaching*. Englewood Cliffs, N.J.: Prentice-Hall.

COOPER, J. M. and GLASSOW, R. B. (1972) *Kinesiology*. St Louis, Mo.: C. V. Mosby.

DURNIN, J. V. G. A. and PASSMOR, E. V. (1967) *Energy, Work and Leisure*. London: Heinemann.

DYSON, G. H. G. (1977) *The Mechanics of Athletics*, 7th edition. London: Hodder and Stoughton.

EAVES, G. (1969) *The Mechanics of Springboard and Firmboard Techniques*. London: Kaye and Ward.

FAIRBANKS, A. R. (1963) *Teaching Springboard Diving* Englewood Cliffs, N.J.: Prentice-Hall.

FREDRICK, A. B. (1966) *Women's Gymnastics*. Dubuque, Iowa: Wm C. Brown.

FREDERICK, A. B. (1969) *Gymnastics for Men*. Dubuque, Iowa: Wm C. Brown.

HAY, J. G. (1973) *The Biomechanics of Sports Techniques*. Englewood Cliffs, N.J.: Prentice-Hall.

HOPPER, B. J. (1973) *The Mechanics of Human Movement*. London: Crosby Lockwood Staples.

JENSEN, C. R. and SCHULTZ, G. W. (1970) *Applied Kinesiology*. New York and Maidenhead: McGraw-Hill

JOHNSON, W. R. (ed.) (1960) *Science and Medicine of Exercise Sports*. New York and London: Harper and Row.

LAWTHER, J. D. (1969) *The Learning of Physical Skills*. Englewood Cliffs, N.J.: Prentice-Hall.

MILLER, D. L. and NELSON, R. C. (1973) *Biomechanics of Sport*. Philadelphia, Pa.: Lea and Febiger.

SLOAN, A. W. (1970) *Physiology for Students and Teachers of Physical Education*. London: Edward Arnold.

STEINDLER, A. (1970) *Kinesiology of the Human Body*. Springfield, Ill.: Charles C. Thomas.

THOMAS, V. (1970) *Science and Sport*. London: Faber and Faber.

TRICKER, R. A. R. and TRICKER, B. J. K. (1967) *The Science of Movement*. New York: American Elsevier.

WELLS, K. F. and LUTTGENS, K. (1976) *Kinesiology, Scientific Basis of Human Motion*. Philadelphia, Pa.: W. B. Saunders.

WILLIAMS, J. G. P. (1965) *Medical Aspects of Sport and Physical Fitness*. Oxford: Pergamon Press.

WILLIAMS, M. and LISSNER, H. R. (1962) *Biomechanics of Human Motion*. Philadelphia, Pa.: W. B. Saunders.

Articles and papers

Floor

AUSTIN, J. M. (1971) 'Cinematographical analysis of the double backward somersault'. *The Modern Gymnast*, 13(3): 22–4 (March).

BORMS, J., DIQUET, W. and HEBBELINCK, M. (1973) 'Biomechanical analysis of the full twist somersault', in CERQUIGLINI, S., VENERANDO, A. and WARTENWEILER, J. (eds) *Biomechanics III*: 429–33. Basel, Switzerland: S. Karger AG.

FORTIER, F. J. (1969) 'Analysis of the reverse lift forward somersault'. *The Modern Gymnast*, 11 (12): 14 (December).

HEBBELINCK, M. and BORMS, J. (1968) 'Cinematographic and electromyographic study of the front handspring', in WARTENWELLER, J., JOKL, E. and HEBBELINCK, M. (eds) *Biomechanics: Technique of Drawings of Movement of Movement Analysis*. Basel, Switzerland: S. Karger AG.

LUNDIEN, E. C. (1966) 'A cinematographic analysis of the backward somersault'. Abstract in *The Modern Gymnast*, 8 (2): 26–7.

ROSENAK, E. (1967) 'The center of gravity in a handstand'. M. S. thesis, University of Wisconsin.

WIENCKE, B. E. (1972) 'The roundoff: a mechanical analysis of a skillfully executed gymnastic stunt'. M. S. thesis, University of Wisconsin.

Vault

BAJIN, B. (1970) 'The vault'. *The Modern Gymnast,* 7 (12): 12–13 (January).

BAJIN, B. (1971) 'Hecht Olympic compulsory vault'. *The Modern Gymnast,* 13 (11): 23 (November).

GEORGE, G. S. (1971) 'The angle of incidence'. *The Modern Gymnast,* 13 (10): 19 (October).

GEORGE, G. S. (1971) 'Long horse angles of incidence specific to reuther board contact'. *The Modern Gymnast,* 13 (12): 22 (December).

Side horse

BLIEVERNICHT, D. L. (1964) 'Side horse leg circles: a cinematographic analysis'. M. S. thesis, University of Wisconsin.

POLACEK, J. L. (1970) 'A cinematographical analysis of loop circles on side horse'. M.S. thesis, Illinois State University.

SARVER, R. E. (1962) 'A cinematographical analysis of the double leg circle on the side horse'. M.S. thesis, Washington State University.

Rings

DUSENBURY, J. S. (1968) 'Kinetic comparison of forward and reverse giant swings on still rings as performed by gymnasts with varying body type'. M.S. thesis, University of Massachusetts.

GUNNY, E. (1971) 'Ringswing'. *The Modern Gymnast,* 13 (8–9): 26 (August–September).

WILSHIN, D. B. (1964) 'An experimental study to determine the force necessary to hold the crucifix on the still rings'. M. S. thesis, Springfield College.

Parallel bars

FURUYA, Y. (1970) 'The study of the swing on the parallel bars: the relationship between the form and the force applied to the bar when swinging on the parallel bars'. *Proceedings* of the Department of Physical Education, College of General Education, University of Tokyo, 5: 13–23. (Reported (1971) in *Index and Abstracts of Foreign Physical Education Literature,* 16: 23.)

MONPETIT, R. and BOULONNE, G. (1969) 'Biomechanical analysis of the backward swing on the parallel bars'. *Movement,* 4: 135.

SULLIVAN, R. M. (1966) 'The forward somersault on the parallel bars'. Abstract in *The Modern Gymnast*, 8(3): 16–17.

High bar

BAJIN, B. (1972) 'Analysis of a piked front salto with half twist dismount from the horizontal bar'. *The Modern Gymnast*, 14 (8–9): 26–7 (August–September).

BOONE, T. (1977) 'Understanding the biomechanics of the over and reverse grip giant swings'. *International Gymnast* (February).

CAPITAO, A. B. (1970) 'A cinematographic analysis of the hecht dismount on the horizontal bar'. M.S. thesis, Eastern Illinois University.

HOUGH, J. E. (1970) 'A film analysis of the glide kip'. M.S. thesis, University of Tennessee.

KUREROV, N. A. and YAZOVSKI, Y. V. (1967) 'The backward somersault with a full twist dismount'. *Teoriya i Praktika Fizicheskoi Kulturi*, 1.

SMITH, J. A. (1976) 'The dynamics of the grand circle on the high bar in men's gymnastics'. *Research Papers in Physical Education*, 3(2): 13–111.

SMITH, J. A. (1978) 'Mechanics in gymnastics – analysis of the high bar back somersault dismounts'. *Proceedings* of the First International Conference on Mechanics in Medicine and Biology, Aachen.

YAMASHITA, N. TAKAGI, K. and OKAMOTO, T. (1971) 'Electromyographic study of the giant swing (forward) on the horizontal bar'. *Research Journal of Physical Education*, 15(2): 93–102 (January).

Asymmetric bars

BOVINET, S. L. (1971) 'The dynamics of the kip on the uneven parallel bars'. PhD. dissertation, University of Illinois.

DROESCHER, E. J. (1972) 'A mechanical analysis of the front somersault between the uneven parallel bars'. M.S. thesis, Springfield College.

General

DORSEY, J. A. (1970) 'Mechanical analysis of gymnastic movement', in *The Magic of Gymnastics*. Santa Monica, Cal.: Sundby Publications.

FLATTEN, K. (1973) 'A biomechanist looks at gymnastic judging – a proposal'. *Journal of Health, Physical Education and Recreation*, 44 (6): 55 (June).

Index